☆ THE ☆
GREAT AMERICAN BURGER BOOK

EXPANDED AND UPDATED EDITION

HOW TO MAKE AUTHENTIC REGIONAL HAMBURGERS AT HOME

GEORGE MOTZ
AUTHOR OF *HAMBURGER AMERICA*

FOREWORD BY ANDREW ZIMMERN

PHOTOGRAPHY BY
KRISTOFFER BREARTON
DOUGLAS YOUNG
GEORGE MOTZ

ABRAMS | NEW YORK

THIS BOOK IS
DEDICATED TO MY MAMA:

Thanks for making
it look so easy

And to the rest of my loving, food-crazy family

CONTENTS

FOREWORD BY **ANDREW ZIMMERN** 8

INTRODUCTION 10

A Brief History of the Hamburger 12

Tools of the Trade 14

Talk to Your Butcher 20

A Word About Hamburger Buns 22

A Word About Cheese 24

Hamburger Architecture 26

THE BASICS 29

The Griddle-Smashed Classic Cheeseburger 30

The Flame-Grilled Burger 36

The Thick Pub Classic Burger 42

REGIONAL FAVORITES

The Great American Burger Map 48

THE MIDWEST 51

The Chicago Cheddar Char (Illinois) 52

The Horseshoe Sandwich (Illinois) 58

The Jucy Lucy (Minnesota) 62

The Gom Cheese Brr-Grr (Indiana) 68

The Sheboygan Brat Burger (Wisconsin) 72

The Poached Burger (Wisconsin) 78

The Butter Burger (Wisconsin) 82

The Loose Meat Sandwich (Iowa) 88

The Olive Burger (Michigan) 92

The Bierock (Nebraska/Kansas) 98

The Guberburger (Missouri) 104

THE WEST 109

The Classic Patty Melt (California) 110

The Bacon-Avocado Toast Burger (California) 114

The Loco Moco (Hawaii) 118

The Teriyaki Burger (Hawaii) 122

The Nutburger (Montana) 126

The Green Chile Cheeseburger (New Mexico) 130

The Tortilla Burger (New Mexico) 136

The Pastrami Burger (Utah) 142

THE SOUTH 149

The Theta Special (Oklahoma) 150

The Fried-Onion Burger (Oklahoma) 154

The Smoked Burger (Texas) 158

The Swine and Cheese (Texas) 164

The San Antonio Beanburger (Texas) 170

The Slug Burger (Mississippi) 176

The Cuban Frita (Florida) 180

The Deep-Fried Burger (Tennessee) 186

The Pimento Cheeseburger (South Carolina) 192

The Carolina Slaw Burger (North Carolina) 198

THE NORTHEAST 203

The Fluff Screamer (Pennsylvania) 204

Korzo's Deep-Fried Lángos Burger (New York) 210

The Gargiulo Burger (New York) 218

The Chester-Rouer (New York) 224

The Steamed Cheeseburg (Connecticut) 230

The Jersey Burger (New Jersey) 236

The Hamburger Parm (Massachusetts) 242

INTERNATIONAL FAVORITES 247

The American Burger, Globally Speaking 249

The Bøfsandwich (Denmark) 250

The Islak (Turkey) 256

The Sloppy Burger (Malaysia) 260

The X-Tudo Burger (Brazil) 266

Burger with the Lot (Australia) 272

TOPPINGS & SAUCES 279

SIDES 305

POSTSCRIPT: THE BEET BURGER (Brooklyn, New York) 320

ACKNOWLEDGMENTS 326

INDEX 328

ANDREW ZIMMERN

Food is good. Food with a story is better. Food with a story you haven't heard before is best of all. Hold that thought.

I stand for many things: I'm a globalist, and a regionalist, but I am first and foremost a New Yorker, which means I was weaned on great hamburgers served in bars, without lettuce or tomato anywhere near them. P.J. Clarke's and J.G. Melon—those were the burger joints my father took me to.

Evenings were always at Melon's. My dad had his Dewar's scotch, into which Billy always poured just the right-size splash of soda. Bobby always gave us a great table. I was in awe of my father at Melon's. He was the master of his domain, saying hi to our friends and neighbors, all the while pounding those crisp, griddled, and rare burgers, served plain. Always with a side of cottage fries that poofed when you cooked them. Lunches were at P.J. Clarke's, taken quickly around the corner from his office. Same style burgers. But Clarke's changed over the years. Went commercial. Sad.

Burgers at Melon's are still beefy and well crusted, they taste of the bowed and broken griddle and the steer. They run their exquisite juices into the bun quickly, so that the bun is always toasted and crisped on the inside to give the burger a fighting chance of holding together. Burgers with my dad were special, the way it is when you're a kid: A rare opportunity to be a man when you're really only a child.

I had my first drink with my dad over a burger. I took my first girlfriend to Melon's for a burger. I got into my first fistfight over a burger there—a girl may have been involved. I got dumped there, too. Twice. Well, more than twice, actually.

I can measure my life in Melon's burgers if I so desire. For me, they're seminal.

Which is why this book is so important. Part historical reference, part recipe book, it doesn't get religious about either. Rather than argue the cultural-authenticity screed, or prattle on about whose burger is better, George Motz celebrates them all, the diversity of America's greatest food obsession. The regional charm and the warm memories speak to all of us, because your burger is in here, too.

I'm a food guy because of my dad, just a paler version of him. I don't live in New York City anymore, so I only get a burger at Melon's a few times a year. Every burger I ever bite into makes me think of my dad; so do the green-and-white checkered tablecloths, those poofy potatoes, and that spinach salad. And those nights I got drunk at Melon's, with all those fabulous women who for some crazy reason went on a date with me—I can see their faces, I can remember their names and how they kissed. Food reminds me of my life; it's powerful that way.

Which is why I've made it my business to eat your burger. The one that does that same thing for you, and thank the sweet baby Jesus that George loves them even more and has collected this incredible all-star cast of archetypes.

Hamburgers are deliciously regional. I am sure there are readers who will dote on the pages dedicated to the Maid-Rite of Iowa in ways I can never fully appreciate. But I know in every fiber of my soul that the Maid-Rite plucks at your heartstrings, and I felt some of that when I had my first one twenty-five years ago.

I remember my first trip to Milwaukee, strolling into Solly's, biting into a butter burger for the first time, a real one, with a dollop of salted butter melting over the hot burger, its slippery-slidey life snuffed out when the top bun was placed on it, trapping happiness on the inside. Its carnal pleasure was released with my first bite. The regional diversity of American foods is the source of our stories, our collective culture, and our communal joy. It needs to be shared.

Look, I've had burgers steamed in Connecticut, fried in Tennessee, enrobed in Hatch green chiles in New Mexico (at Bobcat Bite, before they closed after a near seventy-year run), gone Loco-Moco in Hawaii, and of course Jucy Lucy-ed in Minnesota, where I live now. For my son, that's a real hamburger. For me, it's someone else's story, well, his actually. And when he's old enough to appreciate it I will show him a real burger at J.G. Melon's, because that one's mine.

George Motz is my friend, and I struggled with this assignment; I didn't want it to seem like a favor, or false flattery. But I think this book is a gorgeous rendering of America, seen through the hamburgers of our sons and daughters, of you and yours. These are our stories, all valid, all delicious, all important to someone somewhere.

Through them we see ourselves, and I know you will see yourself in here and be moved, and made joyful, because food with a story works that way. And if you haven't eaten all these burgers or heard of some of them, I am exceedingly jealous, because food with a story you haven't heard about is best of all.

A REGIONAL ODYSSEY

Across America, burger diversity abounds. The unique flavors and textures of our best burgers run deep, and they begin with the regional methods by which the burgers are cooked, well before toppings (both traditional and far-out) are introduced. In my many years of research around the country I have discovered that burgers can be smoked, stuffed, smashed, steamed, deep-fried, grilled, breaded, and poached—very different cooking methods that all produce wonderful results.

A number of cookbooks have been written about the hamburger, arguably America's favorite food. But these tend to focus on the myriad sauces and toppings that can be applied to a standard patty. Rarely is cooking *method* discussed in depth. This cookbook explores the roots of the American hamburger and the steps required to bring regional methods into your home. I have experimented with all the different ways a burger can be cooked, topped, and presented, and I am excited to share my discoveries with the adventurous home cook.

Making great burgers requires careful attention to detail. Even preparing the most basic of burgers takes well-chosen ingredients, a few specific tools, and a bit of practice. I will cover all this territory, and also aim to open your mind to a wide range of regional burger styles. With just a modest amount of trial and error, you should be able to make your regional hamburger dreams come true.

The hamburger should not be a complicated thing. Like a haiku, the best burgers benefit from an imposed limitation of form. The one ingredient paramount over all others is the beef, the foundation of a great burger. The fewer the ingredients and toppings, the more the beefiness of your burger can shine. All the recipes and methods in this book bring the emphasis back to the flavor of beef. So don't look for any tuna burgers (gasp), turkey burgers, or other such variations here. To the burger purist, anything but beef is just a distraction, a gimmick.

For years I have considered it my duty to preserve the sanctity of the All-American burger. With my first book, *Hamburger America*, and my documentary film by the same name, I drew attention to the variety of burger styles in America, their culinary history, and their impact on the evolution of the burger. I took to the road and experienced America's best and most innovative burgers at the source. I met the people who spend just about every day of their lives keeping regional burger traditions alive. I encourage you to explore these places if you can—your burger knowledge will grow with each joint, counter, and stand you visit, as will your appreciation of the people behind one of the greatest foods in America.

Some time has passed since the first printing of this cookbook, and fortunately not much has changed. We've added a few new classics and slightly updated the original recipes, but for the most part we are fortunate that regional burgers are timeless. Two things have changed—we've added an international section, because I've been traveling a lot and have discovered that the American burger has found a place globally. I think you'll like what I've uncovered. And we've lost a few old burger joints mentioned in this book: Guy's Meat Market in Houston and Matt's Drive-In of Butte, Montana. We lament their loss but also realize that this book can serve as a window on history. Keep these traditions alive and make these burgers.

Like great chefs everywhere, many of my hamburger heroes have secret recipes that they will not divulge. Although they have become my friends and some are inclined to confide in me, I prefer to let them keep their secrets. Most of the recipes that I share here are very similar to the originals—with a little license for interpretation—but if you are determined to try the "real thing," hit the road and experience these hamburgers at their place of origin. A burger road trip makes a great vacation and the perfect excuse to get off the interstate and immerse yourself in an America you may have thought already vanished.

I'm not a trained chef, but I am for certain a skilled home cook and a careful observer. I rarely follow recipes, instead cooking the way my mother does, with controlled reckless abandon, using the freshest, most authentic ingredients possible. There are a few basic cooking rules that should not be broken, but beyond that, in my opinion it's best to experiment. Follow your instincts and blaze your own path to flavor. Most of what I know about cooking I learned from my mother and grandmother, but not all of those lessons were about ingredients or techniques. My mother gave me the most important tool for cooking success—*confidence*. That, and the willingness to get into the kitchen every single day and make magic.

Prepare to experience an American culinary road trip in your own home. With *The Great American Burger Book*, explore little-known cooking methods and time-tested recipes from Texas to Wisconsin, Utah to Tennessee, New Jersey to Hawaii. Transport yourself and your family and friends to the unheralded cooktops of a country where the burger is king. —**George Motz**

A BRIEF HISTORY
OF THE HAMBURGER

The history of the hamburger is admittedly a bit nebulous, but for fun we can trace it as far back as the thirteenth-century Mongol Empire. Apparently, the Mongols used to place bits of raw mutton under their saddles as they rode, thus tenderizing the meat for their dinner. Soon after, the Russians adopted a minced version of this dish, added spices, and called it tartar, presumably after the Mongolian people of Central Asia, who were known as Tartars. At this point the basis of the dish shifted from raw mutton to raw beef. It took three hundred years, but the dish eventually made its way across the Baltic Sea to Germany, where the chopped beef was served cooked.

Germans immigrating to the United States in the mid-nineteenth century left out of the Port of Hamburg and sometimes would have to wait months for passage. There they developed a fondness for a local dish, a steak prepared according to the fashion of Hamburg (known outside the city as the Hamburg Steak): chopped beef formed into a patty, cooked, and served on a plate with potatoes and gravy. Upon arriving in New York City, German immigrants found that their Hamburg steak had already made its way to America via Germans who had immigrated before them. It was hugely popular at high-end restaurants like Delmonico's, as well as from food carts found all over Lower Manhattan. News of the Hamburg steak spread, and soon it was available all across America.

It took another twenty to thirty years for the Hamburg steak to be served between two slices of bread, the purest ancestor of the modern-day burger. The many claims to the "invention" of the traditional hamburger hail from different parts of America; all are pretty shaky, but they point to around the same time period: 1885–1900. Some of these claims are linked to transient state fair vendors who reportedly were looking for a way for fairgoers to eat their meatballs and Hamburg steaks on the go. Fletch Davis, the Menches Brothers, Charlie Nagreen, and others also laid claim to the invention, but unfortunately there is little evidence to substantiate those claims. Of course, whoever had the flash of brilliance to first slip a Hamburg steak between two pieces of bread is a national hero. And a genius.

Regardless of what history can or cannot prove, Louis' Lunch in New Haven, Connecticut, has been selling their "hamburger sandwich" since 1900. And today, more than

115 years later, Louis' Lunch still serves the same burger between two slices of white toast. Their claim to be first, however, was recently debunked, thanks to the discovery of an 1894 advertisement in the *Shiner Gazette* for Barny's Saloon in Moulton, Texas. Clear as day, they advertise "Hamburger Steak Sandwiches every day in the week." I love breaking news in hamburger history.

For its first two decades, the hamburger suffered from an image problem. Upton Sinclair's book *The Jungle*, an exposé of the wrongs of the meatpacking industry, caused the general public to be wary of ground beef. The burger was seen as an unsanitary, cheap meal sold to factory workers from dilapidated food carts. But in 1921 one man, Billy Ingram, changed the hamburger world forever when he opened the first White Castle.

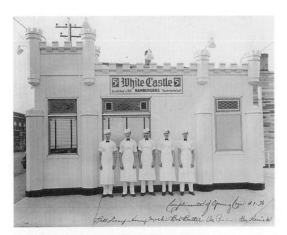

White Castle, opening day, Chicago, Illinois, 1929

White Castle saved the American hamburger from its uncertain future and potential demise. Billy Ingram saw potential in the burger business and partnered with successful Wichita, Kansas, burger-stand owner Walt Anderson. The two cleaned up the burger's image by building small white brick castles with white enamel steel interior walls, staffed by young men in clean uniforms and crisp white paper caps. And the name alone said it all: "White" conveyed a sense of cleanliness, and "Castle" stood for strength.

Perhaps the single most important event in modern hamburger history was White Castle's standardization of the hamburger bun in the early 1920s. Before that, burgers were served on whatever bread the cook could get his hands on. For the next twenty-five years, unless you were copying White Castle's tasty little sliders and its expanding network of burger stands, you were toast.

The Great Depression and World War II altered the burgerscape. Young men went off to war, rationing caused shortages, and burger joints shuttered. But the hamburger managed to survive these hard times through the invention of the machine-formed frozen beef patty and additional menu items like French fries. Following World War II, franchising, the interstate system, and the popularity of the automobile led to the exponential growth of the hamburger business. By the middle of the twentieth century it was clear that the American burger was here to stay—and on its way to becoming a global phenomenon.

TOOLS
OF THE TRADE

The hamburger's humble beginnings are rooted in frugality. The first burgers were made with scraps from higher-end steak trimmings and cooked in pans on street corners for people with very little money. Still today, to make great burgers you do not need fancy cooking tools or expensive kitchen toys, unless of course you are so inclined. The key to producing quality classic-American burgers is simplicity. Here are the basics you will need in your kitchen, or backyard, to make the burgers in this book.

- -
THE SPATULA
- -

You will notice a stiff spatula mentioned in just about every recipe. It will become your most treasured tool, and the thing you'll proudly show off to your friends (the clueless ones with the flimsy spatulas). At a restaurant-supply store it should only set you back five dollars or less. You can spend more, and there are now tools on the market designed for smashing patties (like my very own Smashula). And when I say stiff, I mean stiff. If the spatula you own now bends even a little, chuck it—you will only become frustrated as you make your way through these burger recipes. Get your hands on a 6½-inch (16.5-cm) solid-wood-handled "turner," or spatula. It should have a beveled edge, which you will need for scraping the pan.

THE TONGS

We all own tongs, but you'll need to make sure you have a pair of extra-long steel tongs, free of any plastic or silicone on the business end. You'll be using these tongs in or near hot flames, and you won't want that plastic melting into your precious burgers. Get yourself a pair of 16-inch (40-cm) stainless-steel tongs—again, available at any kitchen-supply store.

THE SCOOP

One of the most misunderstood tools in the hamburger cook's arsenal is the salad scoop (also referred to as a "baller" or "disher," depending on where you're shopping). In order to successfully make consistently sized smashed burgers (the base for many of the burger recipes in this book), you will need a #12 scoop (2½ ounce or 75 g capacity). You may also need a #16 scoop (2 ounce or 60 g capacity) for making sliders. Most of the recipes in this book call for you to shape heaping scoops of ground beef with these dishers, so, in effect, you're almost doubling the capacity (4 ounces or 120 g for hamburgers, 3 to 3½ ounces or 90 to 105 g for sliders).

Unless the cooking technique requires hand-pattying (for grilling and steaming, for example), I always use a scoop to shape burgers. Hand-pattying can lead to compressed meat. With scooping, the meat stays loose, which is the key to the best pan-fried or griddled burgers. Scoop directly from a bowl of loose ground chuck for the best results.

THE FOOD RING

One really cool trick I picked up while observing high-end chefs making lowbrow burgers in their award-winning restaurants was the use of a food ring, sometimes referred to as a "cutter." It's basically a round cookie and biscuit cutter that also works well for forming hamburger patties. The ring allows you to create patties that are uniform in circumference and to shape them with minimal contact. When forming the patties this way, you use only the tips of your fingers (instead of the palms of your hands), which keeps the patties less compressed than the hand-forming method.

THE CAST-IRON SKILLET

THE CAST-IRON FLAT TOP

I've been at this for a while, and, not surprisingly, I own an array of great cast-iron cooking surfaces and pans. But the one I treasure most is my grandfather's 10-inch (25-cm) cast-iron skillet. The pan is almost a hundred years old, has been owned by my family since day one, and has seen some serious Southern cooking, thanks to its South Carolina heritage. My grandfather passed it on to my mother when she was twenty and starting a family on Long Island, and my mother passed it on to me when I moved to New York City at age twenty-one. That skillet has been in appreciative hands since the beginning.

A cast-iron skillet or flat top is a must for your success in the hamburger arts. Absolutely nothing cooks like cast iron. Once you have a cast-iron skillet hot it stays hot, maintaining constant heat better than even the most expensive aluminum pans. Also, because you are working with a porous, seasoned surface, the last burger you cooked will help flavor the next. That's how the old-school burger joints make such tasty burgers. And, unlike the fancy pans out there, a good 12-inch (30-cm) cast-iron skillet will only set you back about forty dollars and it will last forever.

If you've never owned a cast-iron skillet you are in for a treat. The relationship between you and your pan will become one of caring and commitment. You can purchase preseasoned cast iron, which will save you the seasoning process. Then, the more you use the pan, the better it gets. Unlike aluminum, you get out of it what you put into it; take good care of your cast-iron pan and you'll be rewarded with great burgers.

When you need to make more than just a few burgers, it's time to pull out a cast-iron flat-top griddle. Lodge and others make the perfect pro flat top that you can either fit across two burners on your stovetop or toss on your grill outside. Which, by the way, is an excellent solution when you're strapped with cooking burgers on an outdoor propane grill—using a flat top or cast-iron skillet directly on the grill grate will help you produce amazing burgers outdoors. Plus, all that airborne grease produced by the fifty amazing burgers you made for your friends will not end up in your kitchen.

BEEF TALLOW

You will notice throughout this book that I mention that you need to lubricate your pan with beef tallow. There are a few ways to make this happen. The easiest way is to toss some ground beef in your pan just when you are ready to cook. Crumble and cook the beef, allowing the fat to lubricate the pan. Remove the beef and feed it to the dog. You can also buy rendered beef, or tallow, at most good grocery stores or save the beef fat you drained from when you made chili.

PARCHMENT SQUARES

Lately I've begun using a new method for making patties that I call "hand smashing." When you want thin patties but can't smash them thin (in a pan), try hand smashing. The method works well for grilling thin patties or making Jucy Lucys without a patty press. All you need

to do is invest in a pack of precut parchment squares. I've found that 8" × 8" is the perfect size, and I use them all the time. You can also pre-smash a stack of patties, throw them in the fridge, and be prepped and ready to make burgers inside or out.

THE OUTDOOR GRILL

If you have a backyard or outdoor space and are reading this book, chances are you also have a grill. Unfortunately, many of you probably own propane-fired grills, because the results are predictable and passable. But anyone who cooks on propane knows in their heart that the true path to outdoor-grilling magic is charcoal.

And, as with all the tools needed to make great burgers, purchasing a decent charcoal grill will not empty your wallet. A kettle grill or portable hibachi, the standard in outdoor charcoal grilling, can set you back only about a hundred dollars, plus maybe an additional forty dollars for accessories (grill brush, cover, etc.). They also are somewhat portable. Toss your kettle grill in the back of your car, and you can spontaneously grill at a friend's house or on the beach. You cannot do this with a propane grill.

Most valuable, though, is the understanding of open flame and heat that you will develop by cooking with charcoal. I like to think of it this way: Grilling with propane is like driving an automatic car, whereas working with charcoal is much closer to driving stick shift. When you drive stick, you feel the rhythm of the car. When you drive an automatic, your goal is to simply get to your destination. Cooking over charcoal forces you to appreciate the ride.

TALK TO YOUR BUTCHER

Fresh ground beef is the single most important element in any great burger. You care enough about quality burgers to buy this book, so you probably already know this. There are a few simple scientific reasons why fresh beef makes for the very best burgers, but it's the end result that matters—fresh beef tastes better than frozen.

Scientifically, the moment raw beefsteaks are sent through a grinder, liquid is released as the muscle fibers are basically crushed. The clock is ticking, so it goes without saying that the best burgers come from beef that has just been ground. When the Midwestern burger chain Steak 'n Shake opened in 1934, they would grind beef in the dining room in full view of customers to prove this point.

The integrity of ground beef changes dramatically when it has been frozen. When thawed, frozen ground beef will never resemble the loose, plush stuff that comes out of a grinder. The liquid present in the meat forms ice crystals when frozen, and those crystals actually cause damage to the cell structure of the beef, altering its flavor and texture. And, as we all know, good food is all about flavor and texture. But it gets worse—the deeper the freeze, the more extensive the damage, especially upon thawing. Please stick to fresh ground beef, the only path to hamburger success.

If you are grinding at home, pick up an inexpensive hand grinder. The hand-crank models that clamp onto a table edge work well, but if you have a lot to grind it becomes tedious. If you already own a KitchenAid stand mixer, it's time to invest in their dependable grinding attachment. Introduced in the 1940s, the KitchenAid food-grinder attachment has changed very little over the years and costs only about fifty dollars.

Your beef should be kept cold in the fridge until just before you're ready to grind. Beef that has warmed even slightly will begin to soften the fat content, and that in turn will gum up your grinder. The chief culinary advisor at SeriousEats.com, J. Kenji López-Alt, recommends chilling the grinding attachment itself, which is a great idea. Most butchers keep their grinders in their walk-in meat lockers, right by the hanging sides of beef, so Kenji's method is pure common sense. I'm guessing you do not have

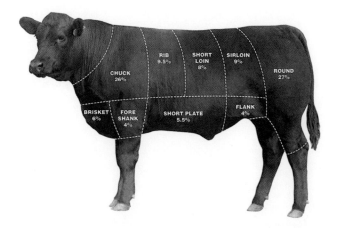

a walk-in at home, so toss your grinder in the fridge about an hour before you plan to grind some beef.

My advice, which comes from years of studying my burger heroes and their methods, is to use chuck steak as a baseline for making great burgers. It's a forgiving cut and the choice for just about every small-town joint and big-city burger pub. Chuck steaks have the perfect muscle-to-fat ratio, especially if ground to 80/20 percent specifications (a scientific method best left to butchers and meatpackers). Certified Angus Beef is a great option to start with; it was the first beef brand in America that was promoted for its consistent marbling and high quality, and it still delivers on that promise today.

If you have not done so already, start a relationship with your local butcher shop. Explain to them that you plan to grind your own beef for burgers, and they should be able to choose a chuck steak that contains marbling close to the ideal 80/20 ratio just by eyeballing it. Ask for a chuck steak, or chuck roast. This is the big steak that butchers sell as pot roast. Experiment by tossing in other cuts of the animal as well, like bits of tasty short rib or brisket (but don't add too much—there's a reason these "less desirable" cuts require longer cooking methods, such as smoking and braising, when cooked on their own). Or ask for their special burger blend: Most butchers, especially those that sell dry-aged steaks, save the trimmings from those cuts and use them in special blends specifically for burgers. It's the way it's been done in butcher shops forever. That's why your butcher's burger blends always taste so damned good.

Certified Angus Beef loves to promote beef and give away cattle-related goodies such as their classic Angus beef cuts poster (see page 334). If you are anything like me, you'll stare at that poster for hours. It's a great way to familiarize yourself with the various cuts of the animal. They also offer an updated version via their website.

A WORD ABOUT HAMBURGER BUNS

After the beef, the bun is unquestionably the most important element to a great hamburger. It can also be one of the most overthought and underappreciated decisions. Buns (or bread) are the delivery system and the only other ingredient necessary to call a burger a burger. A hamburger without a bun is a ground beefsteak, and a bun without a patty is just toast. Put the two together and you have a hamburger. Even without mustard, onions, pickles, or any of the myriad of other condiments available, it is still a burger.

One of my burger heroes, Bill Bartley of Mr. Bartley's Burger Cottage in Cambridge, Massachusetts, describes the bun as "the envelope for the good news that's coming." Bill believes that overthinking the bun is your first mistake. And Bartley's, a tremendously successful Harvard-area burger joint for sixty years, uses large, pillowy, bakery-fresh white squishy buns.

Soft is usually better when seeking out burger buns. Depending on your preference, the recipe buns can be steamed, toasted with butter, or used right out of the bag (assuming the bag was not in a cold place like your freezer). They should be the classic, enriched kind, what I have been referring to for years as the "white squishy bun." Potato rolls/buns also work well (this is actually the bun of choice worldwide for Shake Shack). If you are so inclined, whole-wheat buns will do, though look for the soft ones. Or try using the buns that the Plaza in Madison, Wisconsin, uses: the "half-wheat" bun, or what I like to call the "Look, I'm eating healthy!" bun.

Most of the companies that make organic buns have finally changed their recipes to please the basic tastes of hamburger traditionalists. Not long ago, your only option for a "healthy" burger bun was a ridiculously hard sprouted-wheat bun the size of a grapefruit. Today, health-conscious bakers have found a way to make buns that are very close to the white squishy versions of our dreams.

On the subject of seeded buns, it really makes no difference whether or not your buns have seeds on top (unless of course you are allergic to sesame seeds). Has anyone

ever actually been able to *taste* the difference between seeded and unseeded buns? Not me. Some people do prefer the texture, though.

Toasting hamburger buns before applying beef and condiments is a good idea in most cases. As the late food writer Josh Ozersky once pointed out to me, "Toasting creates a prophylactic barrier between burger and bun." This is true, and toasting will give your burger, loaded with liquid ingredients like mustard, mayo, and grease, a bit more durability. An untoasted bun will disintegrate more rapidly than a toasted one.

A WORD ABOUT CHEESE

It's difficult to imagine a time when the cheeseburger did not exist. But the first condiment to grace a hamburger patty in the beginning was probably raw or cooked onion. It took a good thirty years after the introduction of the hamburger for someone to slip a slice of cheese on a patty as it neared completion. And today, cheese is one of the most recognized accessories in the construction of the perfect burger.

There are varying claims, but it is widely accepted that the cheeseburger first made its appearance in Los Angeles in the late 1920s. It is said that short-order cook Lionel Sternberger at the Rite Spot in Pasadena, California, was the first to melt American cheese on a burger, in 1926. Within just two years, the cheeseburger was on menus all over town. An early printed menu from the now-shuttered South Los Angeles restaurant Odell's lists a cheeseburger smothered with chili in 1928, making the first-cheeseburger claim by Kaelin's of Louisville, Kentucky, in 1934 completely false.

It goes without saying that today the most popular cheese for a cheeseburger, from New York to California, is American cheese. And there's a good reason for this: American cheese is basically engineered for the American burger. It has twice the sodium content of aged cheddar, is inexpensive, and melts perfectly every single time. That said, some don't even consider it cheese, and they are somewhat correct.

In the beginning, American cheese was an unaged cheddar, pasteurized to maintain a lengthy shelf life. It was invented by the son of a Canadian dairy farmer, James Lewis Kraft, for use by the U.S. military. That's right, American cheese (formerly called "pasteurized loaf cheese") was invented by a Canadian. Over the years, the makeup of American cheese has been altered to give it an extraordinary shelf life, mostly due to the absence of microbacteria, the stuff real cheeses thrive on. It's still a dairy product, in the loosest sense of the term, but if you desire "real" cheese on your burger, stick with cheddar, Swiss, or any of the other sliced options. Keep in mind, though, that none will melt like American.

Cheddar is unquestionably the most popular choice of cheese for the burgers found in higher-end restaurants across America. Cheddar works well because, unlike salty American cheese, its funky, sharp quality complements beef grease well. One downside is that most cheddar takes far longer to melt, which can throw off cooking time for your burgers. Bill Bartley, at Mr. Bartley's Burger Cottage in Cambridge, Massachusetts, melts the cheese for his burgers directly on the flat top. He believes that the cheese and patty should not meet until the burger is ready for a bun. He once explained the science to me, saying, "The temperature of the cheese is ambivalent about the temperature of the burger." So true.

Although cheese seems to be inextricably connected to the burger, it is by no means a mandatory condiment. Cheese has been absent from some of the greatest burgers I've consumed. But in most cases, cheese will undoubtedly elevate the burger experience. Cheese also acts as a sort of adhesive to keep other unruly condiments within the burger.

I still love American cheese and its long relationship with the all-American hamburger. In a major twist, Organic Valley and others are now making an American cheese that tastes excellent. Finally, American cheese may be able to shake off its negative image.

HAMBURGER
ARCHITECTURE

We've all been burned by a poorly constructed burger. You know what I mean: the "How do I pick this thing up?" burger, or the burger overflowing with absurd amounts of mismatched condiments. There's also the burger that my friend the food writer Adam Kuban calls the "backslider": a burger whose bun is so hard that the pressure from your first bite causes the contents to slide out the back and onto the plate (or your lap). I've had the misfortune of trying to eat burgers with cold cheese, oversized buns, and limp lettuce and have slogged my way through over-sauced burgers on disintegrating, untoasted, undersize buns. Bad burger architecture is inexcusable and easily avoidable.

A hamburger is a sandwich, and the sandwiches that we return to are the ones we savor down to the last bite. The ones you can't believe you finished because they were that good. A great hamburger should have the same effect. And like a traditional sandwich, the burger's success is in its simplicity. Too much stuff on a burger leads to disappointment or disaster. If you have to use a fork because your burger has fallen apart, I'm sorry, it is no longer a burger. Remember, the basic design of the hamburger makes it a hand-held food—it is the ultimate portable meal. And if you find yourself merging onto the 405 in Los Angeles while taking a bite of your In-N-Out Double Double Animal Style with your free hand, you've just proven my point.

The original American hamburger was not a gut-busting, overdressed two-fister. It was a tiny thing—less than 2 ounces (60 g) with a single flourish of chopped onion grilled into the patty. Cheese didn't even enter the picture until a full three decades after the first burgers were conceived. Over the years, the standard size of the classic cheeseburger has grown, but if you pay attention, you'll see that the mom-and-pop shops that have been around for almost a century are still keeping their burgers at a manageable size.

When constructing the burgers in this book, be mindful of the final stage: consumption. As incredible as some burgers look with mounds of condiments and a crazy stack of patties, think about the mouths you're about to feed and what can actually fit into

them. I would much rather eat four basic classics than one enormo burger dreamed up by someone who would never eat it.

Finding the right balance of elements, meaning the ideal burger architecture, is a matter of experimentation. You may need to fail first to succeed. When your bacon cheeseburger tastes like a bacon sandwich, it's time to reconsider the ratios. It may sound obvious, but your hamburger should taste like beef first, enhanced by the addition of select ingredients. Also, take your cues from history. Look at the success of the burgers in the various regions of America over the decades. There's a reason that a burger with nothing but soft Wisconsin butter on it has been continuously served for more than seventy-five years. Simplicity trumps all.

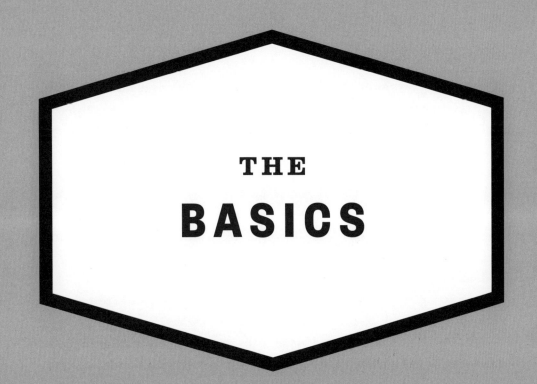

THE
BASICS

THE GRIDDLE-SMASHED CLASSIC CHEESEBURGER

I'm not going to mince words here: This is my favorite way to make a burger. And there's a reason for it. In cooking, in most cases, the simplest path leads to the greatest rewards. With this astonishingly straightforward recipe, you will be transported to a time long ago, before the highway system, frozen patties—hell, even before the invention of the patty press and the conventional hamburger bun. That's because this is the way burgers were made in America at the very beginning. The progenitor of every burger we have ever seen, made, or tasted. This is the burger to which all other burgers can trace their DNA, and arguably it's the most significant burger style in American culinary history.

Short-order chefs at the dawn of the burger age were not interested in brioche buns or bacon marmalade. They were interested in one thing only—speed. The typical burger stand in the 1910s and 1920s was just that: a place to stand and order a burger on the street. Often, stands were outfitted with four or five stools, so turnover was key. The faster a burger was served, the faster that stool became free. These stands used cast-iron skillets and flat steel to cook on, because they were inexpensive. And the method of squashing a ball of meat evolved because the ball was a uniform unit of measure, and the automated patty press was some years off in the future.

In the beginning, it was common practice to grab a handful of rolled balls of beef, scatter them on a flat top, and whack them into the shape

Boo Koo Hamburgers, Harlingen, Texas, 1939

of patties with a spatula. There are still places today that continue the method—White Manna in New Jersey, Crabill's in Ohio, and Wedl's in Wisconsin, to name a few.

The practice of smashing balls of beef seems instinctively wrong, especially to those who have always been told that a burger will lose its "precious juices" should the patty be manhandled. Let go of what you think to be true and start smashing. The method contains some crazy magic that just seems to work. The result is a burger that evokes the same response every single time I serve it (especially from people of a certain age)—"This is the burger I remember."

Even long after all of those corner stands had vanished, and White Castle had expanded greatly and begun freezing patties, many mom-and-pop shops continued smashing burgers on flat tops. The places that keep this tradition alive have helped preserve a distinctly American form of gastronomy.

THE GRIDDLE-SMASHED
CLASSIC CHEESEBURGER

**MAKES 8 CHEESEBURGERS
OR 14 SLIDERS**

EQUIPMENT

A seasoned cast-iron skillet or flat top

A stiff spatula

A #12 salad scoop for full-size cheeseburgers, #16 salad scoop for sliders
(see Note)

THE BURGER

8 potato buns (make sure to get the
right-size buns for either cheeseburgers or sliders)

Beef tallow (rendered beef fat; see
page 18)

2 pounds (about 1 kg) fresh-ground
80/20 chuck

Salt, for seasoning

American cheese, thinly sliced (preferably fresh-sliced cheese from
your deli counter, not prepackaged
"singles")

THE TOPPINGS

Not here, my friend. This classic American cheeseburger *needs no condiments*. So, before you add anything,
taste it. There's a good chance you'll
become a purist like me on the spot.

Note: If you're making sliders, the
patties will take slightly less time to
cook than is listed here. Watch for red
liquid to know when to flip.

1 Toast the buns in a preheated cast-iron skillet or on a preheated flat top (see next column) and set them aside.

2 Preheat the cast-iron skillet over medium heat (or a flat top to medium) and add a tablespoon or two of the beef tallow. Use the spatula to spread the fat, coating the cooking surface.

3 Put the ground chuck in a mixing bowl. Using the salad scoop, form balls of beef (they should be heaping scoops), placing them on the heated skillet as you go. Each ball should have about 3 inches (7 cm) of space around it. (Depending on the size of your cooking surface, you may only be able to cook 2 or 3 burgers at a time.)

4 Sprinkle a generous pinch of salt on each ball of beef and then, using a stiff spatula, press them down, hard. Don't be afraid, press harder! Press each ball until it's a wide patty, just a bit larger than the bun it's about to meet. Here's the trick, though: Once the patties are flat, step back and don't touch them again. Let them cook for 2½ minutes or until reddish liquid begins to form on the surface of the patties.

5 Flip them *once* and resist the temptation to press the patties again.

6 Add a slice of cheese to each patty and let them cook for another 2 minutes.

7 Remove the burgers from the skillet and place them on toasted white buns.

THE VERY BEST WAY TO TOAST A HAMBURGER BUN

Most people don't give much thought to hamburger buns, and that's a mistake. In many cases (but not all), the bun should be toasted. But stay away from the toaster! Use my pan-toasting method instead. That way the only thing getting toasted is the part of the bun touching the burger patty. The part that you grab should stay soft and fluffy. Here's how:

EQUIPMENT
A seasoned cast-iron skillet or flat top
A stiff spatula (recommended)

INGREDIENTS
Butter, softened
Hamburger or slider bun of your choice

1 Preheat the cast-iron skillet over medium heat (or a flat top to medium).
2 Spread a thin, even layer of butter on both halves of the bun. Too much butter and the bun soaks it up; too little and it won't toast. Just enough and the bun will crisp to a tasty golden brown.
3 Once the pan is hot, place the bun halves on it, butter side down.
4 Monitor the buns every minute or so, so they don't burn. Use the spatula to remove from the pan, not your hands, to avoid damaging or squishing the bun.
5 Repeat with the remaining buns.

THE FLAME-GRILLED BURGER

Cooking over direct flame is one of the most difficult ways to make a hamburger. One of the reasons so many of the hamburgers made a hundred years ago were cooked on flat tops was simply because the results were predictably good. Squash a ball of beef on a skillet and reap the rewards of the path of least resistance. I also would imagine that way back then, lighting a big charcoal grill and flame cooking at small burger stands and joints throughout America would have been pretty dangerous.

But we all know that a burger cooked on a flame grill is a very different burger.

It's easy to master the skillet-cooked burger. Grilling a burger on open flame requires more dedication to the craft, more time, more equipment, and a willingness to fail. That's because cooking on an outdoor grill can be very unpredictable. The grill master is at the mercy of uneven temperatures, depending on the type of coals used and where those coals are in relation to the grilling grate. Even the weather can be a factor. The outdoor propane grill solves a few of these issues, but if you really want to experience a flame-cooked burger, super-hot charcoal is the only way to go.

There's something fundamental and primal in our desire to harness fire and grill. "The greatest advantage to cooking over flame is the grilled flavor," Michael Ollier, corporate chef at Certified Angus Beef®, told me once, adding with a smile, "I crave that." It's a flavor that you cannot ever

achieve cooking on a flat top or by any other method. Chef Ollier explained the science behind this perfectly: "The fat that drips onto the coals becomes airborne, flavoring your burgers."

The keys to grilling success are high heat and confidence. Get your coals super hot and your tools, patties, and condiments ready to go, and you'll be all set up to grill like a pro. When family and friends are hovering around you at the grill, waiting for magic, it may feel like there's a lot at stake. Just follow the recipe below for the classic grilled cheeseburger—and remember, practice makes perfect.

THE FLAME-GRILLED BURGER

MAKES 8 BURGERS

EQUIPMENT

A 3½-inch (9-cm) food ring or round
   cutter

Parchment paper

A charcoal chimney

Charcoal briquettes or lump charcoal

A charcoal kettle grill, hibachi, or
   similar

A stiff spatula (with a long handle)

THE BURGER

2½ pounds (about 1 kg) fresh-ground
   80/20 chuck

Salt and coarse black pepper, for seasoning

8 soft white buns

THE TOPPINGS

8 thick slices American, cheddar, or
   any other good melting cheese

Green-leaf lettuce

1 or 2 red beefsteak tomatoes, sliced

1 medium Vidalia or Walla Walla onion,
   sliced

1 Divide the beef into 8 equal portions (5 ounces/140 g each).

2 Place the food ring on a cutting board or clean surface lined with parchment paper and add a portion of beef. Gently press the beef into the ring to create a perfectly round patty. (I use the ring for consistent thickness, but you can eyeball the size if you prefer. Both methods work fine. Just be sure not to over-press the meat—you want it to maintain a somewhat loose grind.)

3 Return the patties to the fridge to chill until you're ready to grill (hey, that rhymes).

4 Using the chimney starter, light the charcoal. When coals are ready, transfer them to the grill, making sure that the bottom vent is open. Spread the coals out, leaving a small space on one side (as a rest spot in case things get too hot in there).

5 Place the grate over the coals and, using a grill brush, scrape off any residual buildup from your last grilling adventure. Cover the grill and make sure that the top vent is wide open. Give your grill grate a chance to heat up—you don't want to plop raw burger patties onto a lukewarm grill. That grate should be ridiculously hot!

6 At this point, and not before, season both sides of your patties with a liberal amount of salt and pepper. Salting too early will bind the muscle fibers together and make your burgers tough (yuck).

7 Place the patties on the hot grill grate, cover the grill, and leave them alone. Allow the patties to cook for about 5 minutes. The cooking time can vary depending on environmental and equipment factors, so you'll have to use your best judgment here. Chef Michael Ollier from Certified Angus Beef put it best when he told me, "Let the burger speak to you." If you understand this statement, you're probably drinking too much at the grill. But seriously, with experience comes wisdom—the burger will actually *tell* you when it's time to flip. One good visual cue is when you see red liquid start to form on the uncooked surface of the burger. Go ahead and take a peek just shy of 5 minutes.

8 This would be a good time to toast your buns. Toast them indoors using a skillet on your stovetop (page 33), or toast them with butter in a small cast-iron skillet, directly on the colder side of the grill.

9 Cook the second side (again, untouched and covered) for an additional 4 minutes. With about 1 minute to go, top each patty with a slice of cheese and cover the grill. As the burgers finish cooking, slide them to the cooler rest spot section of the grill, away from the hot coals. Once all your burgers are done, remove them from the heat and allow them to rest for 1½ minutes. The internal temperature of the burgers should be about 143°F (62°C) for medium-rare.

10 Top the toasted buns with the lettuce, tomato, and onion slices, or your condiments of choice. (I love a good, crisp slice of onion on my grilled burgers, as well as mustard, pickle, and sometimes mayonnaise.) Transfer the patties to the toasted buns and serve.

THE THICK PUB CLASSIC BURGER

Sometimes biting into a big, juicy burger is what you crave, but for the most part the burgers of our forefathers were not like this. In the first few decades following the appearance of the hamburger in America, it remained small and smashed thin on a flat top, making for crisped edges. Although this method produced a profoundly tasty burger, the one thing it lacked was the copious juices you might find in, say, a steak.

The best pub-style thick patties come from bars that have a tiny flat top, in certain cases still located near or just behind the bar to quickly feed tipsy patrons. Some of the best I've ever had were thick, hand-pattied beauties that were just about the only thing on the menu (other than alcohol). Places like the Mo Club in Missoula, Montana, and Paul's Tavern in Dubuque, Iowa, evoke a simpler time when the burger truly was an egalitarian meal and the poor man's steak. But it's New York City that leads the pack in pub burgers per capita. There are still many pubs in the five boroughs peddling nothing more than burgers and booze, some of them more than a hundred years old. In my opinion, the best pub burger experiences can be found at New York City classics such as J.G. Melon, P.J. Clarke's, and Donovan's Pub.

All of these burgers have a few important things in common—they are all hand-formed, cooked on a flat-top griddle, and left untouched while cooking. And unlike the Griddle-Smashed Classic (page 32), these burgers are seared like a steak to create a tasty griddle char that seals in those precious juices.

J.G. Melon, New York City   The Mo Club, Missoula, Montana

With the right elements you can create a burger that tastes exactly like a juicy steak. And since the true taste of beef will dominate, this would be a good time to experiment with different cuts of beef blended into the grind. For just about every burger in the book, 80/20 fresh-ground chuck is the call, but if you're grinding your own (see page 20), you should consider adding a small amount of short rib, brisket, rib eye, or even dry-aged cuts to make the flavor profile more complex. Now that's something you can't do with a steak.

Seasoning is also key when making the thick pub classic. Salt and pepper are staples for a reason—simplicity allows the beef to shine. Please resist the misguided temptation to put things into your ground beef like onions, eggs, and spices. Unless of course meatloaf is your endgame, or the Cuban Frita (page 182), a very different type of burger. I recommend seasoning only the *outside* of your burger just moments before the patty hits the griddle.

THE THICK PUB CLASSIC BURGER

MAKES 4 LARGE BURGERS

EQUIPMENT

A 4½-inch (12-cm) food ring or round
   cutter

Parchment paper

A cast-iron skillet with a lid

A stiff spatula

A small or medium-size metal bowl

Note: This burger will create a good
amount of smoke and airborne grease.
Be sure you have a good vent/hood
over your stovetop, or be ready with
some open windows.

THE BURGER

2 pounds (about 1 kg) fresh-ground 80/20
   chuck (or your beef blend of choice)

Beef tallow (rendered beef fat; see
   page 18)

Salt, for seasoning

Ground black pepper (optional)

4 seeded white buns, toasted (see
   instructions, page 33)

THE TOPPINGS

8 slices American or cheddar cheese

Mayonnaise

Green-leaf lettuce (optional)

1 or 2 red beefsteak tomatoes, sliced
   (optional)

1 medium Vidalia or Walla Walla onion,
   sliced

Cooked bacon (optional but prevalent
   on pub burgers; recipe on page 294)

Dill pickle spears (on the side)

1 Divide the beef into 4 equal portions (8 ounces/250 g each).

2 Place the food ring on a cutting board or clean surface lined with parchment paper and add a portion of beef. Gently press the beef into the ring to create a perfectly round patty. (I use the ring for consistent thickness, but you can eyeball the size if you prefer. Both methods work fine. Just be sure not to over-press the meat—you want it to maintain a somewhat loose grind.)

3 Add some beef tallow to the cast-iron skillet, using the spatula to spread the fat, and crank it up to medium-high heat. When the pan just starts to smoke, it's ready.

4 At this point, and not before, season both sides of the patties with a liberal amount of salt (and pepper, if desired). Salting too early will bind the muscle fibers together and make the burgers tough (not good).

5 Place the patties in the hot skillet—they should sizzle loudly when they hit the pan—and cook for 5 minutes without disturbing them. The goal here is to sear the burgers, sealing in the juices. When you see red liquid start to form on the uncooked surface of the burgers, it's time to flip them.

6 Reduce the heat to medium and cook the second side for an additional 5 minutes (do not disturb them while cooking). With about 1 minute to go, add two slices of the cheese to each patty and cover with a large domed lid or small metal bowl.

7 Remove the burgers from the heat and allow to rest for 1½ minutes. The internal temperature of the burgers should be about 143°F (62°C) for medium-rare. Transfer to the toasted buns and serve with mayo, lettuce, sliced tomato, onions, bacon (if using), and pickles on the side.

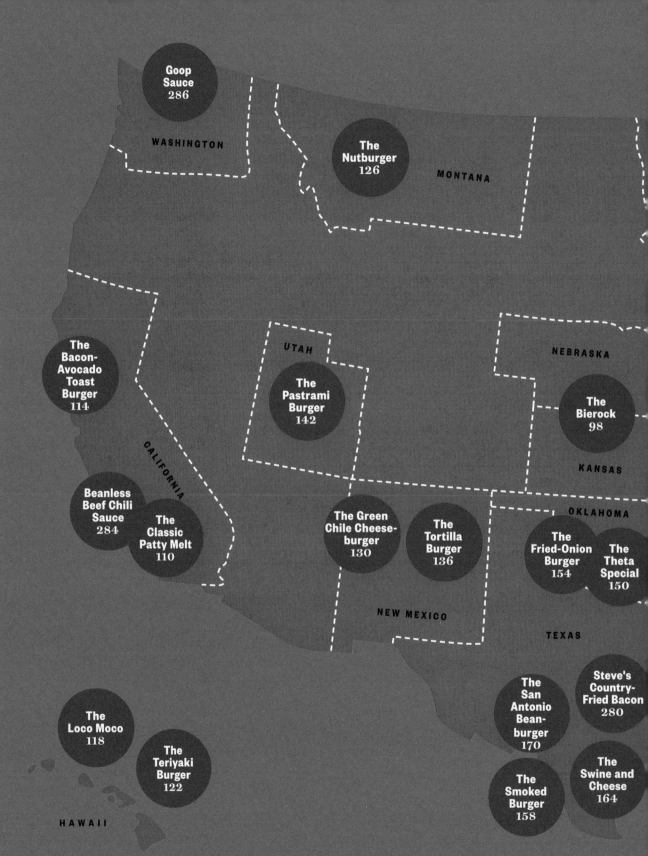

Goop
Sauce
286

WASHINGTON

The
Nutburger
126

MONTANA

The
Bacon-
Avocado
Toast
Burger
114

UTAH

The
Pastrami
Burger
142

NEBRASKA

The
Bierock
98

CALIFORNIA

KANSAS

Beanless
Beef Chili
Sauce
284

The
Classic
Patty Melt
110

The Green
Chile Cheese-
burger
130

The
Tortilla
Burger
136

OKLAHOMA

The
Fried-Onion
Burger
154

The
Theta
Special
150

NEW MEXICO

TEXAS

The
Loco Moco
118

The
Teriyaki
Burger
122

HAWAII

The
San
Antonio
Bean-
burger
170

Steve's
Country-
Fried Bacon
280

The
Smoked
Burger
158

The
Swine and
Cheese
164

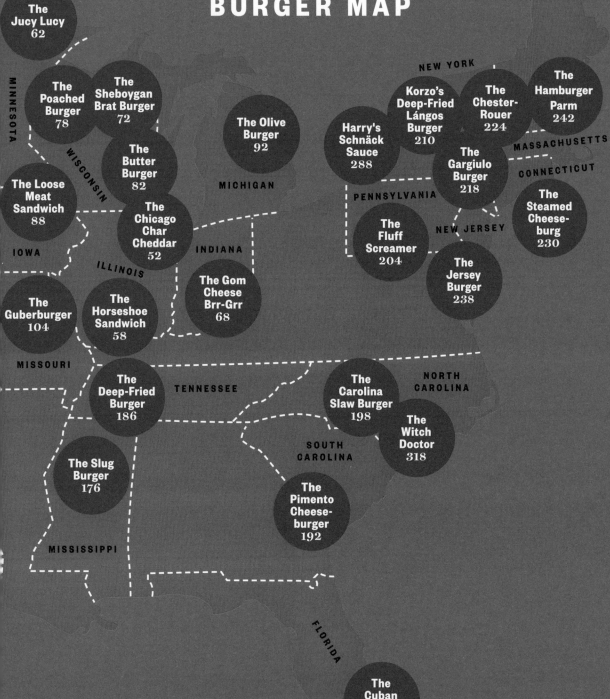

THE GREAT AMERICAN BURGER MAP

The Jucy Lucy
62

The Poached Burger
78

The Sheboygan Brat Burger
72

The Olive Burger
92

Korzo's Deep-Fried Lángos Burger
210

Harry's Schnäck Sauce
288

The Chester-Rouer
224

The Hamburger Parm
242

NEW YORK

MINNESOTA

The Butter Burger
82

WISCONSIN

The Gargiulo Burger
218

MASSACHUSETTS

CONNECTICUT

The Loose Meat Sandwich
88

The Chicago Char Cheddar
52

MICHIGAN

PENNSYLVANIA

The Steamed Cheese-burg
230

IOWA

ILLINOIS

INDIANA

The Fluff Screamer
204

NEW JERSEY

The Gom Cheese Brr-Grr
68

The Guberburger
104

The Horseshoe Sandwich
58

The Jersey Burger
238

MISSOURI

TENNESSEE

The Deep-Fried Burger
186

The Carolina Slaw Burger
198

NORTH CAROLINA

The Witch Doctor
318

The Slug Burger
176

SOUTH CAROLINA

The Pimento Cheese-burger
192

MISSISSIPPI

FLORIDA

The Cuban Frita
180

REGIONAL FAVORITES

THE MIDWEST

ILLINOIS

ILLINOIS

THE CHICAGO CHAR CHEDDAR

The char cheddar is one of those burgers where you must get the ingredients and method right or you just don't have a char cheddar. Unlike the load of ingredients in the Danish bøfsandwich, or the complicated process of the Hawaiian teriyaki burger, this is a very simple burger. And if executed well, it is heavenly.

All the char cheddars I've had have been in Chicago and the surrounding suburbs, but one of the very best has been at the Des Plaines, Illinois, hot dog stand Paradise Pup. The forty-year-old stand is better known for its quick-serve Chicago char dogs "dragged thru the garden," but I also go for the burgers.

The key element to a char cheddar is the cheddar cheese spread. But not just any kind. For this recipe you'll need a very special spread invented by a Wisconsin tavern owner: Merkts cheddar spread. This is not the crazy, overprocessed, gas station cheese goo most of us avoid; in fact, this is the stuff that industrial-strength cheese was modeled after. This is cold pack cheddar.

Do not confuse spreadable cold pack cheese (also known as "pub" or "crock" cheese) with Velveeta or Cheez Whiz. The latter are, well, not very cheesy. They are made to taste like cheese and melt like cheese, but they actually contain very little cheese. They are also processed using heat,

Paradise Pup, Des Plaines, Illinois

where, as the name implies, cold pack cheese does not. The result is a cheese that tastes like real sharp cheddar. And unlike a hard slice of refuse-to-melt cheddar, it's already "melted." You'll never go back to sliced cheddar again.

The other important element of the char cheddar is the char. This burger *must* be cooked over an open flame to get that flavor. Use your charcoal grill, make your patties thick, and you are almost there. Next, and finally, to make it a true Paradise Pup char cheddar, add only caramelized Spanish onion. No other toppings are necessary—they will only interfere with the smoky, beefy, hot cheddar experience you are about to have.

THE CHICAGO CHAR CHEDDAR

MAKES 4 CHEESEBURGERS

EQUIPMENT

4 (8-inch/20-cm) parchment paper squares

A 4-inch (10-cm) food ring or round cutter

Charcoal briquettes or lump charcoal

A charcoal chimney

A charcoal grill

A grill brush

A long-handled grill spatula/turner

THE BURGER

1 pound (about 500 g) fresh-ground 80/20 chuck

Salt, for seasoning

4 sturdy seeded buns

Caramelized Onions (using Spanish onions; recipe at right)

1 (12.9-ounce/366 g) tub Merkts cheddar spread or any other cold pack pub cheese spread, softened (30 minutes at room temperature)

1 Divide the beef into 4 equal portions (4 ounces/125 g each).

2 Place the food ring on a cutting board or clean surface lined with parchment paper and add a portion of beef. Gently press the beef into the ring to create a perfectly round patty. (I use the ring for consistent thickness, but you can eyeball the size if you prefer. Both methods work fine. Just be sure not to over-press the meat—you want it to maintain a somewhat loose grind.)

3 Repeat with the remaining portions of beef.

4 Put the patties in the fridge until you're ready to grill.

5 Using the chimney starter, light the charcoal. When coals are ready, transfer them to the grill, making sure that the bottom vent is open. Spread the coals out, leaving a small space on one side (as a cooler rest spot in case things get too hot in there).

6 Place the grate over the coals and, using a grill brush, scrape off any residual buildup. Cover the grill and make sure that the top vent is wide open. Give your grill grate a chance to heat up—you don't want to plop raw burger patties onto a lukewarm grill. That grate should be ridiculously hot!

7 At this point, and not before, season both sides of your patties with a liberal amount of salt and pepper. Salting too early will bind the muscle fibers together and make your burgers tough (yuck).

8 Place the patties on the hot grill grate, cover the grill, and leave them alone. Allow the patties to cook for about 2 minutes. The cooking time can vary depending on environmental and equipment factors, so you'll have to use your best judgment here. A good visual cue is when you see red liquid start to form on the uncooked surface of the burger, then it's time to flip. Take a peek just shy of that 2-minute mark.

9 Flip the patties and split the bun halves, placing the buns facedown on the coolest side of your grill grate. Check them after *maybe* 1 minute (be careful: charcoal grills run hot!) and take them off the grill once toasted.

10 Cook the second side of your patties (again, untouched and covered) for an additional 2 minutes.

11 Assemble the burgers: Place a pile of the caramelized onions on the heel of the toasted bun and top with a grilled patty. Then smear your top bun with a big dollop of cheddar spread and bring it home. That's it! Eat and repeat.

CARAMELIZED ONIONS
Makes enough to top 5 burgers

3 tablespoons (45 ml) olive oil
2 medium Vidalia or Walla Walla onions
3 pinches salt
¼ cup (60 ml) white wine
1 tablespoon salted butter

1 Preheat a skillet over medium heat and add the olive oil.
2 Slice the onions into fairly thin rings or strings and add to the skillet, stirring to coat with oil and continuing to stir and poke and pat and move around until onions become limp, about 6 minutes.
3 Add salt and stir to incorporate.
4 Add the wine and raise heat to high for 1 minute or so, stirring constantly until liquid evaporates, then return to medium and add butter, stirring until melted.
5 Cook, turning the onions in the pan frequently for another 10 minutes or until they are nicely golden brown and caramelized (i.e., they look awesome). Remove from the heat and set aside.

ILLINOIS

THE HORSESHOE SANDWICH

The Horseshoe Sandwich is the pride of Illinois. Its invention is credited to Chef Joe Schweska at the Leland Hotel in Springfield, Illinois, in 1928. As legend has it, a hungry hotel guest came in as the kitchen was closing one night and Joe quickly put together a meal using things he had left on hand. That same day, Joe's wife, Elizabeth, had given him a recipe for classic Welsh rarebit (an eighteenth-century British cheese sauce) to use in a menu special. When Schweska created an open-faced sandwich for the guest using thick toast, a slice of hot ham, a mound of shoestring fried potatoes, and a cascade of cheese sauce, a legendary sandwich was born.

In its original iteration the sandwich was made with a piece of ham cut into the "U" shape of a horseshoe, and the shoestring fries represented the nails. At some point, two burger patties replaced the horseshoe of ham, making the default of this dish a hamburger plate. In some parts of Illinois today you can find versions replacing beef patties with pulled pork, chicken, turkey, corned beef, and more.

The recipe for the cheese sauce is Chef Schweska's original one-hundred-dred-year-old recipe. Apparently, he was very open about his work and shared the recipe with anyone who asked. You'll notice the recipe calls for beer as an ingredient. When the horseshoe was born, it was during Prohibition, so the chef likely had to use "near beer" (a very low-alcohol malt brew created by breweries to get through those dark days) in his cheese sauce. A traditional rarebit sauce calls for ale.

THE HORSESHOE SANDWICH

MAKES 2 SANDWICHES

EQUIPMENT

8 (8-inch/20-cm) parchment paper
  squares

A seasoned cast-iron skillet

A deep skillet for frying

THE SANDWICH

1 pound (500 g) fresh-ground 80/20
  chuck

Salt, for seasoning

4 slices thick white Pullman bread,
  toasted

3 cups (710 g) frozen shoestring fries,
  deep-fried

Chef Joe Schweska's Original Sauce
  (recipe follows)

1 Divide the beef into 4 equal portions
(4 ounces/125 g) each.

2 Then, using 2 squares of parchment
paper, hand-smash each portion between
the sheets until they are about $\frac{1}{8}$ inch
(3 mm) thick.

3 Heat one skillet over medium-high heat
and, when it is starting to smoke, add 2 of
the patties.

4 Add a pinch of salt to each patty in the
pan and cook for about 3 minutes.

5 Flip and cook for another minute, then
repeat with the other 2 patties.

6 Place 2 toasted bread slices each onto
2 wide plates.

7 Place 1 patty on each slice of toast
(4 total) and cover with cooked shoestring
fries.

8 Just before serving, pour a good helping
of Joe's cheese sauce over each plate.

CHEF JOE SCHWESKA'S ORIGINAL SAUCE

Makes enough for 2 horseshoe sandwiches

½ cup (1 stick/115 g) butter
¼ cup (30 g) all-purpose flour
1¼ cups (300 ml) milk
½ teaspoon dry mustard
1 tablespoon Worcestershire sauce
8 ounces (225 g) high-quality cheddar
cheese, shredded
1 teaspoon salt
½ teaspoon cayenne pepper
4 ounces (120 ml) beer (preferably ale or
pilsener), at room temperature

1   Melt the butter in a medium saucepan over low heat, then add the flour and whisk constantly.

2   When the flour mixture is a little toasted (it will smell almost nutty), after about 2 minutes, slowly add the milk. Whisk constantly until all the lumps are gone (do not let it boil).

3   Add the dry mustard, Worcestershire, cheese, salt, and cayenne pepper, still whisking constantly while cooking, until the cheese melts and a smooth cream sauce remains.

4   Stir in the beer just before serving.

A WORD ABOUT FRIES

This recipe calls for French fries, and they're integral to the dish. Most cookbooks will show you how to make perfect fries at home, but let's be honest here—that's not a simple task for even the above-average home cook. Most of the fries you eat and love at restaurants start as frozen fries. Your best course of action (other than timing a delivery from your favorite local restaurant with award-winning fries) is to get a bag of frozen from the grocery store, ignore the bake-in-oven method, and deep-fry them. You've got this—just fill a pot with cooking oil and fry 'em up just like the pros (see the Red Chile Potato Chips, page 314). The result will be, well, restaurant fries!

MINNESOTA
THE JUCY LUCY

In 1953, a man walked into Matt's Bar, a neighborhood watering hole in the south side of Minneapolis, and asked the bartender, Matt Bristol, to make him "something special." Back then many corner taverns were outfitted with tiny flat top grills just behind the bar, alongside the cash register and bottles of booze. Bartenders were expected to mix drinks and flip burgers, and food was offered as a way to nourish the regulars and keep them from heading home for dinner. In some cases the food that bars offered back then was free, used as an incentive for customers to stick around and keep drinking.

That day in 1953, Matt produced a burger that was truly special. He took two of the bar's thin, preformed burger patties, placed a slice of American cheese between them, and tossed it on the flat top. When the man bit into the concoction he allegedly exclaimed, "That's one juicy Lucy!," and a legend was born. It was such a hit that Matt put his new invention on the menu (incorrectly spelling it "Jucy," a quirk that is still reflected on the old menu board today). Versions of the Jucy Lucy can be found in most major American cities, and a handful of other establishments in and around the Twin Cities have created their own versions. Matt's Bar still serves well over five hundred of the cheese-stuffed beauties on a busy day.

The method by which a Jucy Lucy is constructed should not be taken lightly. This burger is more ambitious than your usual casual tavern fare and its preparation has more in common with a science experiment. All of the elements have to be precisely handled. Get one aspect wrong and pay dearly. A chef friend of mine once offered the Jucy Lucy at his New

Matt's Bar, Minneapolis, Minnesota

York City restaurant as a special, only to appear in the dining room in a panic looking for me. Turns out his first batch of untested Jucy Lucys were exploding on the grill, spewing hot cheese everywhere. With the Jucy Lucy, success is in the details.

If you are lucky enough to get to Matt's for a Jucy Lucy, you'll find that it may be one of the only burgers in America that comes with a warning. That's because if you bite into your burger too quickly you will suffer second-degree burns from the molten cheese exploding in your face (I've been a victim). You will frequently overhear the waitstaff ask, "Have you had one before? Let it cool down before you take a bite." And if these warnings are not enough, staff shirts have the phrase "Fear the Cheese" printed on the back.

If I haven't completely scared you out of trying this recipe, let's do some weird science. Let's make a Jucy Lucy at home. The traditional recipe calls for good-old American cheese, but you should experiment with any cheese you desire. Pepper Jack, cheddar, and blue cheese all work well. But in my opinion, there's really nothing quite like a Jucy Lucy with hot, dripping, yellow American cheese.

THE JUCY LUCY

MAKES 8 BURGERS

EQUIPMENT

A medium-size mixing bowl

A #16 salad scoop

A hand patty press, set to make ¼ inch
(just under 1 cm) thick patties

Parchment paper cut into 6-inch
(15-cm) squares

A seasoned cast-iron skillet or flat top

A stiff spatula

A toothpick

Note: The Jucy Lucy may require
practice. It wasn't until my third
attempt that I was successful. If at first
you don't succeed, get back in there
and show that Jucy Lucy who is boss.
And remember: Fear the Cheese.

THE BURGER

2 pounds (about 1 kg) fresh-ground
80/20 chuck

8 slices yellow American cheese

Beef tallow (rendered beef fat; see
page 18)

8 classic soft white buns, toasted (see
instructions, page 33)

Salt, for seasoning

THE TOPPINGS:

2 medium Vidalia or Walla Walla
onions, diced

Butter

Dill pickle chips

1 Place the ground beef in the mixing bowl and, using the salad scoop, shape the meat into balls. These should be level scoops (about 2-ounce/60-g balls) to create 16 balls total. Set aside.

2 Line the hand patty press with a square of parchment, place a ball of beef in the center, place another square of parchment paper on top, and press the lid of the patty press down hard until you've made a patty. Leave the formed patty in the parchment paper for now. Each Jucy Lucy requires two patties so repeat this step until all the balls of meat have been pressed.

3 Once you have 16 patties between parchment squares, it's time to start building Jucy Lucys: Take two patties and remove one sheet of parchment paper from each. Take a slice of American cheese and fold it in half, then in half again so you have 4 quarter-slices of cheese in a stack. Place this stack in the center of one of the patties. Line up the second patty on top of the first, parchment paper side up. You should now have a parchment "sandwich" with meat and cheese in the center. Using your fingers, pinch the edges of the two patties together through the parchment paper, making sure to seal the entire perimeter of the burger. This seal is very important. The patty will look more like a clam than a hamburger patty at this stage.

4 Repeat this process until all the patties are cheese-filled clam-shaped patties.

5 Preheat the cast-iron skillet over medium heat (or a flat top to medium) and add some beef tallow. Use the spatula to spread the fat, coating the cooking surface. Once hot, add the onions to the pan and a pat of butter. Cook, stirring occasionally, until the onions are golden brown. Transfer to a bowl.

6 Place 2 or 3 pickle chips on each of the toasted bottom buns and set aside.

7 Remove the remaining parchment paper from two or three of the cheese-filled patties and place them in the same skillet used for the onions. Add a dash of salt to each patty and cook for 4 minutes before flipping.

8 The next step involves a bit of science: Flip the burgers gently, taking care not to break the meat or let the cheese escape. Using the toothpick, poke a tiny hole in the center of each burger. Don't poke all the way through—only through to the cheese layer. This will allow the steam that has built up inside the patty to escape without draining the burger of its precious cheesy contents. If you skip this step, the burgers will explode and ruin your day. I'm not kidding.

9 Cook the patties for another 4 minutes. Spoon some cooked onions on the bottom halves of the buns and place a cooked patty on top of each. Serve immediately but be sure to warn your guests to let the burgers cool for a few minutes before taking a bite.

46

INDIANA

THE GOM CHEESE BRR-GRR

There is a 120-year-old ice cream parlor in the center of downtown Columbus, Indiana, called Zaharakos, which serves a sticky, burger-like concoction with a very rich history. That burger is called the Gom Cheese Brr-Grr.

The Gom is technically in the cheeseburger family, but it's not really a cheeseburger. It's a sandwich with hamburger qualities (much like the Loose Meat Sandwich of Iowa, page 88, or the chopped cheese of East Harlem, New York). What disqualifies the Gom is that there's no formed beef patty. This is a loose, tasty, hot mess, and you are going to love it.

Imagine the union of a sloppy joe and a grilled cheese sandwich and you are almost there. The slop is kind of sticky, or "gommy" (which comes from an old Dutch slang word), and is loaded with tasty spices and a bit of brown sugar and molasses. Interestingly, in Indiana, the sloppy joe is sometimes referred to as a "Dutch Hamburger." Also, it has not been confirmed, but it's possible that the Zaharakos brothers may have invented the original sloppy joe.

Zaharakos staffs soda jerks in uniform who operate original turn-of-the-century soda fountains, and there is an enormous, original Welte Orchestrion player organ from 1908 at the rear of the restaurant. When someone cranks it up, all conversation comes to a halt. The place is a historic gem that belongs in the Smithsonian. In 2007 Zaharakos closed briefly but was saved by local businessman Tony Moravec. Tony made his fortune selling a very well-known diaper rash cream called Boudreaux's Butt Paste

Zaharakos, Columbus, Indiana, circa 1915

(if you've had babies, you've probably used Boudreaux's). Tony is a national treasure. He is absolutely not getting rich from the burger business, and we are all better for it. A guy who invents baby butt rash paste takes the money and uses it to revive a local landmark *and* recover the original organ to put back in the restaurant: my hero.

46

THE GOM
CHEESE BRR-GRR

MAKES 4 CHEESEBURGERS

EQUIPMENT

A seasoned cast-iron skillet

A wooden or rubber spatula

THE BURGER

1 tablespoon olive oil

½ medium sweet or white onion,
   finely diced

1 pound (about 500 g) fresh-ground
   80/20 chuck

1 teaspoon garlic powder

1 tablespoon chili powder

¾ cup (180 ml) water

2 tablespoons tomato paste

1½ teaspoons light brown sugar

1 tablespoon molasses

A few dashes of hot sauce

Salt, for seasoning

4 slices American cheese

8 slices white sandwich bread,
   toasted

1 Drizzle the olive oil in a cast-iron skillet and heat over medium heat.

2 When the oil begins to smoke, add the onions, stir, and cook until they're translucent, about 3 minutes.

3 Next, add the beef to the onions. Chop and stir, cooking until crumbly and there's no pink in sight, 3 to 4 minutes.

4 Remove the skillet from the heat and drain most of the fat by tilting the pan and scooping out the excess liquid. Discard this (or save for future burgers!).

5 Return the skillet with the beef and onion to medium heat and add the garlic powder, chili powder, water, tomato paste, sugar, molasses, and hot sauce. Mix thoroughly. Add salt to taste.

6 Cook until "gommy," or sticky, but not too wet.

7 While your meat is getting good and gommy, prepare some toasted bread and set aside.

8 Finally, FOLD IN the cheese—don't stir!

9 Serve immediately on toasted bread.

WISCONSIN

THE SHEBOYGAN BRAT BURGER

Sheboygan, Wisconsin, is the epicenter of bratwurst culture in America (this was made official by a judge in 1970, barring all other claims). The city even holds an annual multiday festival called Brat Days, which was canceled for twelve years from 1966 to 1978 due to "excessive rowdiness." Brats, beer, and rowdiness . . . now that's my kind of party!

For those unaware, the American bratwurst is a very large, fresh, uncured pork sausage. Wisconsin has a large number of residents of German ancestry, and this sausage is a direct result of that heritage. Although German in name, the American version is a bit different. Germany is home to more than a thousand varieties of sausage, or *Wurst*, but the version that has made its mark on Wisconsin is the bratwurst from southern Germany. The sausage may date back as far as the fourteenth century and is similar in flavor to the famous Nuremberg bratwurst. The Nuremberg is a very thin sausage, and legend has it that in medieval times the family of a jailed political dissident made them small enough to fit through the keyhole of his dungeon door. When this sausage traveled to the American Midwest, it grew in size, substantially, and can now be found at every ballpark, backyard party, and street fair.

The traditional way to enjoy a bratwurst in the Sheboygan area is with dill pickle chips, grainy mustard, and raw onion on a hard roll called

Newspaper ad for first Bratwurst Day, Sheboygan, 1953

a *semmel* (similar in profile to a Kaiser roll but more oblong in shape, not round). Some add ketchup (but shouldn't), and others prefer sauerkraut. If you are at the Charcoal Inn, you can get a brat burger, which involves the standard toppings (no sauerkraut) and the classic Wisconsin burger topping, soft butter. The brat burger is a collision of two fantastic foods from the Dairy State.

Two more rules apply, however: never, ever in Wisconsin will you find cheese on a brat. The Visit Sheboygan website even has a brat oath that includes the line ". . . I will deny all temptation to engage in inter-relations between brat and cheese . . ." Also, all brat burgers and brats must be cooked over charcoal. Wisconsin is one of the only places in the United States I have found where restaurants and counters have *indoor* charcoal grill setups designed for year-round grilling, usually in the spot where you might find a flattop. In this part of the world brat lovers will not compromise.

THE SHEBOYGAN
BRAT BURGER

MAKES 4 BURGERS

EQUIPMENT

4 (8-inch/20-cm) parchment paper
 squares

A 4-inch (10-cm) food ring or round
 cutter

Charcoal

A charcoal chimney

A charcoal grill

A grill brush

A long-handled grill spatula/turner

A very sharp knife

THE BURGER

1 pound (about 500 g) fresh-ground
 80/20 chuck

4 fresh Wisconsin bratwurst in natural
 casing

Salt, for seasoning

4 sturdy kaiser rolls or hard rolls

THE TOPPINGS

Grainy, German-style mustard

Dill pickle chips

1 white or sweet onion, sliced into thin
 rings

Salted butter, softened

1 Divide the beef into 4 equal portions (4 ounces/125 g each).

2 Place the food ring on a cutting board or clean surface lined with parchment paper and add a portion of beef. Gently press the beef into the ring to create a perfectly round patty. (I use the ring for consistent thickness, but you can eyeball the size if you prefer. Both methods work fine. Just be sure not to over-press the meat—you want it to maintain a somewhat loose grind.)

3 Using the chimney starter, light the charcoal. When coals are ready, transfer them to the grill, making sure that the bottom vent is open. Spread the coals out, leaving a small space on one side (as a cooler rest spot in case things get too hot in there).

4 Place the grate over the coals and, using a grill brush, scrape off any residual buildup. Cover the grill and make sure that the top vent is wide open. Give your grill grate a chance to heat up—you don't want to plop raw burger patties onto a lukewarm grill. That grate should be ridiculously hot!

5 While the grill is heating, prepare your brats: Using a very sharp knife, slice the bratwurst lengthwise in half, but don't cut all the way through.

6 Flip the split sausage over and, in one move, gently pull the casing off the sausage. Set aside.

7 At this point, and not before, season both sides of your patties with the salt. Salting too early will bind the muscle fibers together and make your burgers tough (yuck).

8 Place the patties and split sausages on the hot grill grate, cover the grill, and leave them alone. Allow them to cook for about 2 minutes. The cooking time can vary depending on environmental and equipment factors, so you'll have to use your best judgment here. A good visual cue is when you see red liquid start to form on the uncooked surface of the burgers; then it's time to flip. Take a peek just shy of that 2-minute mark.

9 Flip the patties and sausages. Meanwhile, add the split rolls, placing them facedown on the coolest side of your grill grate. Check them after *maybe* 1 minute (be careful: charcoal grills run hot!) and take them off the grill once toasted.

10 Cook the second side of your meats (again, untouched and covered) for an additional 2 minutes.

11 Assemble the burgers: To the heel (bottom) of the roll, add a good dollop of the mustard followed by the cooked patty, the bratwurst (sliced in half to fit on the burger), some pickles, and the raw onion. Smear a healthy dollop of soft butter on the inside of the crown (top) of the roll, and place on top. You are now cleared to eat like a Wisconsinite.

WISCONSIN

THE POACHED BURGER

This is unquestionably one of the most peculiar burgers I've come across in America, and also one of my favorites. When journalists ask me questions like, "What's the craziest topping you've ever had on a burger?," I always feel like they're missing the point. In my burger universe, crazy comes in the form of method, not added stuff. I've seen burgers deep-fried, smoked, steamed, and beyond—all with fantastic results. And then I met the poached burger.

As far as I know, there's only one place to get this burger: Pete's Hamburgers in Prairie du Chien, Wisconsin. It's nowhere near a major city and is a destination burger stand if ever there was one. Pete's is really far away from anything, has a relatively short season (open weekends only, April to October), but show up on a beautiful sunny summer day and there will be a line down the block (which moves very quickly).

The burgers at Pete's are cooked in a way I've never seen before: They're boiled, or basically poached, in a large, low-lipped tank of water. Pete's, which started serving burgers over a hundred years ago, does not refer to their burgers as poached: It's just the way they've been doing it all these years. Pete Gokey had a small lunch cart and would cook burgers on a griddle at fairs and circuses in town. "He noticed the patties that sat too long would dry out," Pete's grandson Paul Gokey told me once. "So he started pouring water on them to keep them moist." From then on Pete found that the best way to cook burgers was in shallow, hot water. And you know the saying, if it ain't broke, don't fix it.

Pete's Hamburgers, Prairie du Chien, Wisconsin

Just as with the Steamed Cheeseburg (see recipe, page 232), moisture and beefiness become pronounced when hot water is introduced. And unlike burgers cooked in a skillet, poaching doesn't make a grease-splattered mess of your kitchen. As a taste enhancer, the Gokey family keeps an enormous mound of sliced onions in the center of the water pan, which naturally flavors the liquid and, in turn, the burgers. When an order comes in, a Gokey grabs a patty—along with a scoop of the limp, hot onions—and slips it onto a fresh bakery roll. To complete the flavor profile, the Gokeys offer a squirt of horseradish mustard. Another strange thing about Pete's is that cheese is nowhere to be found there. Strange, of course, because Wisconsin is the Dairy State. My guess is that there's really no way to melt cheese on this burger, and you'll be fine without it. The lack of cheese forces you to focus on the simplicity of the elements at play: beef, onion, and mustard.

If the idea of poaching burgers sounds unappetizing and silly, your instincts are clearly functioning properly. Fortunately, though, your instincts are wrong. There would not be a line down West Blackhawk Avenue in Prairie du Chien if the poached burger were anything but amazing.

THE POACHED BURGER

EQUIPMENT

A mandoline slicer

A large (3-quart/3-L) frying or sauté
    pan

A stiff spatula

A large baking dish

THE BURGER

2 pounds (about 1 kg) fresh-ground
    80/20 chuck

2 large sweet Vidalia, Walla Walla, or
    Spanish onions, sliced paper thin
    on a mandoline slicer

1 tablespoon salt

8 sturdy bakery hamburger buns,
    sliced

THE TOPPINGS

Horseradish or spicy mustard
    (optional)

1 Preheat the oven to 250°F (120°C).

2 Divide the beef into 8 portions (4 ounces/
125 g each) and roll into balls. Place in a
container in the fridge until ready to cook.

3 In a large frying pan, bring about 1 inch
(2.5 cm) of water to a boil.

4 Reduce the heat to medium and add half
of the thin-sliced onions and the salt. Cover
and cook for 5 minutes or until the onions
are translucent.

5 Add 4 beef balls to the onion water,
evenly spaced. Using the stiff spatula, press
the balls into ¾-inch (2-cm) thick patties
and cook for 5 minutes, then flip them and
cook for another 5 minutes.

6 Meanwhile, place the sliced bakery buns
in an oven-ready dish or pan, cover with
foil, and heat in the oven for about 7 minutes or until soft and warm.

7 When the burgers are cooked through,
serve on the warmed buns with a scoop of
the onions from the cooking water and a
dollop of the horseradish or spicy mustard,
to be completely true to Pete's.

8 Repeat steps 4 through 7 to cook the rest
of the burgers. You may need to add a little
more water to the pan before adding the
rest of the onions. Let them cook for a few
minutes more before adding the rest of the
raw beef balls, so the water gets hot again.
Also, note that your second batch is going
to taste better than your first, because the
water is now seasoned with the rendered
beef fat from the first batch.

THE BUTTER BURGER

Before I made the film *Hamburger America*, very few people had heard of the butter burger of Wisconsin. Even in the nearby city of Chicago it was perceived as a sort of burger mythology, a thing that "may" exist. That's because the concept of the butter burger sounds absurd. Who uses butter as a hamburger condiment? Why, some clever folks in the great dairy state of Wisconsin, of course!

What many in the state refer to as a butter burger simply involves swiping the inside of a toasted bun with a thin coat of pure, creamy Wisconsin butter. But to truly experience this unique American burger you'll need to visit the place where it was invented: Solly's Grille in Glendale, Wisconsin. Solly's, which is near Milwaukee, started adding butter to their burgers in the 1930s and the idea caught on.

If you make the pilgrimage to the small, yellow, double-horseshoe-shaped Formica counter at Solly's, you can indulge in a few butter burgers—but these burgers are not for the lactose intolerant. That's because Solly's still uses 2 to 3 tablespoons of soft local butter *per burger*. That's right, and if you are lucky enough to have that hot burger delivered to your spot at the counter fast enough, you will get to experience biting into butter that is still in a semi-solid state. And you may also catch yourself doing just what I did on my first visit to Solly's—dipping the last bite of your burger back into the pool of butter on your plate. You will quickly discover that whatever guilt you harbored during your first bite has dissipated by your last.

Solly's, Milwaukee, Wisconsin

Anything can be added to a butter burger—the standard lettuce and tomato are sometimes included—but by far the best way to enjoy a butter burger is the simple way, with butter and stewed onions only.

Onions are always great on a burger, whether they are fried, raw, stewed, or sautéed. There's something about the combination of beef, butter, salt, and onion that is hard to beat. Glenn Fieber, my butter burger hero at Solly's Grille, has a recipe for stewed onions so secret that only a handful of family members have been entrusted with its details. I think I may have gotten close with the following recipe, but for the real thing you'll have to plan a trip to Milwaukee. Glenn's version has the consistency and flavor of the onions in French onion soup, and that's a good thing.

The butter burger is one of the most difficult burgers to make at home, simply because you'll have a hard time trying to convince your brain to put that much butter on a burger. It's kind of like trying to cut your own hair, or self-surgery—always better when someone else does it. Find a friend and make some butter burgers!

THE BUTTER BURGER

MAKES 8 BURGERS

EQUIPMENT

A seasoned cast-iron skillet

A stiff spatula

A medium-size mixing bowl

A #12 salad scoop

THE TOPPINGS

Glenn's Stewed Onions, My Way (recipe
follows)

THE BURGER

Beef tallow (rendered beef fat; see
page 18)

2 pounds (about 1 kg) fresh-ground
80/20 chuck

Salt, for seasoning

1 cup (2 sticks/225 g) high-quality
salted butter, softened to room
temperature (try to source authentic
Wisconsin butter for best results)

8 soft white buns, toasted (see instructions, page 33)

1 Make the stewed onions according to the recipe directions.

2 Preheat the cast-iron skillet over medium heat and add some beef tallow. Use the spatula to spread the fat, coating the surface.

3 Put the ground beef in the mixing bowl and use the salad scoop to make balls of beef, placing them on the heated skillet as you go. Each ball should have about 3 inches (7 cm) of space around it.

4 Sprinkle a generous pinch of salt on each ball of beef, then using the stiff spatula press them down hard. Once they are flat, don't touch them again. Let them cook for 2½ minutes or until reddish liquid begins to form on the surface of the patties.

5 Flip them *once* and let cook another 2 minutes without touching.

6 Remove the pan from the heat and place the patties on the toasted buns, with a heaping spoonful of stewed onions on top.

7 Using a wide spreading knife or a spoon, spread what seems like far too much (nearly 2 tablespoons) of the soft butter directly onto the inside of the bun top—*not directly on the burger*. If you apply the butter to the hot patty directly, it will immediately slide off and onto your foot.

8 Carefully marry the buttered bun to the burger, consume immediately, and stop thinking. Just enjoy it.

GLENN'S STEWED ONIONS, MY WAY
Makes enough to top 8 butter burgers

I love that Glenn has secrets. But I also love his stewed onions and wish he'd give me the recipe. Alas, he won't (cue Glenn's infectious chuckle). So here is an approximation of what I think Glenn does when he's sequestered back there in the kitchen at Solly's.

3 tablespoons (45 ml) olive oil
2 medium Vidalia or Walla Walla onions, diced
2 tablespoons butter
½ cup (120 ml) dry white wine
1 cup (240 ml) beef broth
1 teaspoon ground black pepper
Salt, to taste

1 Heat the oil in a saucepan over medium heat.
2 Add the onions and butter to the pan, stirring until the butter is melted.
3 Add the wine, stir, cover, and cook for about 10 minutes or until the onion is translucent.
4 Add the beef broth and pepper, cover, and reduce the heat and simmer. Cook for 20 minutes.
5 Uncover and bring to a boil, evaporating the remaining liquid. Stir until the onions are soft and liquid-free, about 2 minutes. Remove from the heat and set aside until you're ready to top some butter burgers.

IOWA

THE LOOSE MEAT SANDWICH

If you find yourself rambling through Central Iowa, you will discover that traditional burgers are not the ground-beef sandwich of choice. Throughout much of the state, and even in a few pockets of Kansas and Ohio, the loose meat sandwich is what you are looking for. Sometimes it's referred to as a Tavern, or a Maid-Rite (which is also a regional chain), or in Kansas as a Nu-Way (a local Wichita chain). Whatever you call this sandwich, it's technically not a burger, but it shares so many burger-like characteristics, and is so damned satisfying, that I include it here.

True to its name, the loose meat sandwich is basically an unformed hamburger. It's served on a bun with mustard and pickles, but the difference lies in the preparation of the beef. Instead of a standard patty, ground beef is crumbled and steamed with nothing but salt added. Much of the fat drains off and you are left with a lean pile of pebbled beef. Once married to a bun that has been doped with condiments, it becomes a sort of sloppy joe without the slop. It is a very straightforward sandwich—one where the flavor of beef shines.

The most popular loose meat sandwich in Iowa is the Maid-Rite. And one of the original purveyors of the sandwich, going all the way back to 1928, is Taylor's Maid-Rite in Marshalltown, Iowa (do not confuse this Maid-Rite location with the chain of the same name). Since the crumbled

Taylor's Maid-Rite, Marshalltown, Iowa

beef sits in a huge steaming trough behind the counter, service is lightning fast. No joke, when you order at Taylor's, your loose meat sandwich arrives at your spot on the counter in a matter of seconds. It's served with a spoon to scoop up the beef that has spilled out of the sides.

You'll get a kick out of the recipe that follows and may chuckle at its simplicity. This is one of those "burgers" where the sum is far greater than its parts, in this case only one basic ingredient—beef.

THE LOOSE MEAT SANDWICH

MAKES 6 SANDWICHES

EQUIPMENT

A seasoned cast-iron skillet

A wooden spoon

A perforated serving spoon

THE BURGER

1 pound (about 500 g) fresh-ground
   80/20 chuck

Salt, for seasoning

THE TOPPINGS

6 classic soft white hamburger buns

Yellow mustard

Dill pickle chips

1 Preheat the seasoned cast-iron skillet over medium heat. Add the beef and, using the wooden spoon, crumble the beef as it cooks, as if you were preparing ground beef for tacos.

2 Once the meat is pebbly, kick the heat up to medium-high and cook for about 4½ minutes, until just after the pink leaves.

3 Drain most (but not all) of the fat by tilting the pan and pushing the beef to the high side. You need to save this fat in the fridge for future use!

4 Prepare, or "dope," the hamburger buns with a squirt of mustard and 2 or 3 pickle chips on the bottom half of each bun. Set aside.

5 Use the perforated spoon to scoop up a pile of meat, draining off any remaining fat, and press onto a prepared bun. Repeat with the remaining meat and buns.

MICHIGAN

THE OLIVE BURGER

Michigan has made its fair share of contributions to the gastronomic legacy of America. It gave birth to the breakfast cereal business, with both Post and Kellogg taking up residence in Battle Creek. Unquestionably some of the best Cornish pasties outside of Cornwall, England, can be found in the Upper Peninsula of Michigan. And Michigan is one of the largest producers of asparagus and tart cherries in the United States.

But perhaps the strangest burger invention never to venture outside Michigan state lines (but profoundly popular within them) is the olive burger. The claims to the invention are varied depending with whom you consult. Some credit the Greek-owned Olympic Broil in Lansing with the creation of the first olive burger in the 1960s, but others say it was made much earlier at an original Kewpee Hotel Hamburgs location in Grand Rapids (which later became the flagship of a local burger chain called Mr. Fables). John Boyles, former owner of Mr. Fables, told me, "My father started putting olives on burgers in the 1930s when Mr. Fables was a Kewpee." The restaurant sold a burger called the Deluxe Sandwich that came with a special mayonnaise and chopped olives. "Everybody called it the Olive Burger," John explained.

Regardless of who first put olives (and nothing else) on a burger, I've had several great olive burgers all over the west side of the state, where this delicacy reigns. One of my personal favorites is the classic version at the Peanut Barrel in East Lansing. Like many other restaurants in West Michigan, theirs is a simple blend of chopped green salad olives and mayo placed

Kewpee Hotel Hamburgs, Grand Rapids, Michigan

on the burger with no other condiments, and none are needed. But when I had the ear of Smashburger founder Tom Ryan (a Michigan native) he told me, "No, no, no, the best came from Mr. Fables in Grand Rapids [now out of business]. They didn't make a mayo-olive sauce," Tom went on, "a special mayo was on the bun and the chopped olives were on the burger."

Tom *loves* the olive burger and emphasized that the best olives to use are the store-bought pimento-stuffed variety. He explained that when the olives are not premixed with the mayo the result is a very different olive burger. In the test kitchen we tried both approaches and enjoyed the Mr. Fables version just a bit more. And it's hard to argue with Tom, who has a Ph.D. in food science and flavor chemistry.

You should try both versions before you decide which you prefer. From what I've learned, some restaurants use a bit of the brine from the olives to add some complexity and tang to the sauce. Both versions place major emphasis on the olive. Keep it simple and avoid cheese or any other toppings. You'll want that briny flavor to radiate, just as it does in Michigan.

THE OLIVE BURGER

MAKES 8 BURGERS

EQUIPMENT

A small- and a medium-size mixing
  bowl

A seasoned cast-iron skillet

A stiff spatula

A #12 salad scoop

THE BURGER

Beef tallow (rendered beef fat; see
  page 18)

2 pounds (about 1 kg) fresh-ground
  80/20 chuck

Salt, for seasoning

8 soft white buns, toasted (see instructions, page 33)

THE TOPPINGS

Olive-Mayo Mix

¼ cup (60 ml) mayonnaise

1 cup (155 g) pitted green olives,
  chopped until coarse but not minced

or

Mr. Fables-Style Mix

¾ cup (180 ml) mayonnaise

1 teaspoon sugar

1 teaspoon brine from jar of olives

1 tablespoon distilled white vinegar

1 cup (155 g) pitted, pimento-stuffed,
  green olives, coarsely chopped
  (do not mince)

1 If you're making the Olive-Mayo Mix, do so now by combining the mayo and chopped olives in the small mixing bowl. Set aside. If you're making burgers the Mr. Fables way, combine the mayonnaise, sugar, olive brine, and vinegar in the small mixing bowl (alternately, use 1 tablespoon of rice wine vinegar in place of the sugar, olive brine, and vinegar).

2 Preheat the cast-iron skillet over medium heat and add some beef tallow. Use the spatula to spread the fat, coating the cooking surface.

3 Place the ground beef in the medium-size mixing bowl and, using the salad scoop, form balls of beef, placing them on the heated skillet as you go. Each ball should have about 3 inches (7 cm) of space around it. (You may only be able to cook 2 or 3 burgers at a time.)

4 Add a generous pinch of salt to each ball of beef and, using the stiff spatula, press them down hard to create wide patties. Once the patties are flat, don't touch them again. Let them cook for 2½ minutes or until reddish liquid begins to form on the surface of the patties.

5 Flip the patties *once* and don't press them again. Cook for another 2 minutes or so.

6 Transfer the cooked burgers to the toasted bottom buns and top with either a heaping scoop of the Olive-Mayo Mix or the Mr. Fables–Style topping from step 1. Add the top buns and serve immediately.

NEBRASKA/KANSAS

THE BIEROCK

Unless you're from Kansas or Nebraska, you've probably never heard of a bierock (a small pastry filled with cooked ground beef). Nebraska has a restaurant chain devoted to the bierock called Runza, and variations on this meat-filled treat are ubiquitous around the world. In Louisiana they are *kolaches*, in Michigan and Cornwall, England, they are the Cornish pasty, in Poland and Ukraine they are pierogies, and Argentina has a version we know as the empanada. The most mainstream of all descendants of the bierock is the Hot Pocket, the microwavable portable meal found in many gas stations, 7-Elevens, and grocery store freezer aisles throughout America. The list goes on, and similarities abound, but they all descend from the same basic Volga German recipe brought to the Heartland in the late 1800s.

Today's best examples of the bierock can be found in tiny cafes throughout rural Kansas and Nebraska, and in the homes of Midwestern families of German descent who have kept this tradition alive. The bierock usually makes appearances at family gatherings, on the potluck table, or at church fundraisers.

Sometimes also referred to as the cabbage burger the bierock is one of my favorite interpretations of the hot-beef-pocket-as-burger. It actually predates the American hamburger by many decades. A traditional bierock has only three ingredients: crumbled beef, cabbage, and onion, but I've had a few excellent versions that included American cheese. It's a simple combination of ingredients wrapped in a basic dough and baked. And much like a hamburger, it was designed to be handheld and eaten on the go. A bierock is

small enough to fit in your pocket and was most likely the perfect lunch for field and farm workers in a time long ago.

The bierocks I make are the simple, traditional version, but with cheese added as a sort of glue to the loose, crumbling contents. When you take your first bite of a bierock you will be transported to a hardscrabble time in America, when the best comfort food came from the mother country.

THE BIEROCK

EQUIPMENT

A large mixing bowl or standing mixer with a dough hook or paddle attachment

A small saucepan

A clean kitchen towel

A clean, smooth surface for kneading and rolling out the dough

A sharp knife or pizza cutter

A large seasoned cast-iron skillet

A wooden spoon or spatula

A slotted spoon

Parchment paper

A baking sheet

THE DOUGH

4 cups (500 g) all-purpose flour, plus more for dusting

1 package (¼ oz/7 g) active dry yeast

½ cup (1 stick/115 g) butter

1 cup (240 ml) whole milk

⅓ cup (65 g) sugar

1 teaspoon salt

2 large eggs

Olive oil for greasing

THE BURGER

2 tablespoons olive oil

1 tablespoon butter

1 medium yellow onion, finely chopped

4 cups (scant 1 L) white cabbage, shredded

1 pound (about 500 g) 80/20 ground chuck

Salt and ground black pepper, for seasoning

8 slices American cheese

Note: If making dough isn't your thing, a great "cheat" here is to go to your local pizzeria and buy some of their dough. Or pick up fresh-made pizza dough at the supermarket.

1 Make the dough first and leave enough time for it to rise (1 hour or until doubled in size). In a large bowl or standing mixer add 2 cups (250 g) of the flour and the yeast.

2 In a small saucepan, heat the butter, milk, sugar, and salt over low heat until warm (120°F or 50°C). Add the mixture to the bowl with the flour and yeast, and then add the eggs. Beat on low speed until the contents are combined, about 1 minute, then raise the speed to medium-high for 3 minutes.

3 Reduce the speed again, or mixing by hand, slowly add the remaining 2 cups (250 g) flour until a stiff dough forms.

4 Dust the work surface with flour, transfer the dough to the work surface, and knead for about 8 minutes. When the dough is smooth and elastic, transfer it to an oiled mixing bowl, lightly oil the top of the dough, cover with the clean kitchen towel and set in a warm spot to rise (about 1 hour or until doubled in size).

5 Meanwhile, preheat the cast-iron skillet over medium heat and add the olive oil and butter. Once hot, add the onions to the skillet, stir, and cook until translucent.

6 Add the cabbage to the skillet with the onions, stir to combine, and cook until wilted but not brown.

7 Crumble the ground beef into the skillet over the cabbage and onion mix. Stir continuously, breaking up the meat as you go, and cook until the beef is brown and pebbly (about 7 minutes). Add salt and pepper to taste. Remove from the heat and set aside. Preheat the oven to 375°F (190°C).

8 When the dough has risen, transfer it to the floured work surface, punch flat, and roll out to ⅛ inch (3 mm) thick. Using a knife or pizza cutter, cut the dough into 4-inch (10-cm) squares. You may have scraps that you can knead back together and roll out again to make more squares.

9 Using the slotted spoon to drain the fat, scoop the beef-and-vegetable mixture into a bowl.

10 Scoop about 2 tablespoons of the beef mixture onto the center of each square of dough. Next, top each pile of meat with a single square of American cheese, folded into quarters and placed on top in a stack.

11 Pull all four corners of each dough-square together, pinching them shut, then bring the folded edges together and pinch those into the center around the filling to seal it closed like a dumpling.

12 Place them, pinched side down, on a parchment paper–lined baking sheet and bake for 25 minutes or until the tops are just brown.

MISSOURI

THE GUBERBURGER

As far as I can tell, the Guberburger was not invented in Sedalia, Missouri, in 1947. It certainly became popular there, thanks to Lyman Keuper, owner of the Wheel Inn Drive-In, who supposedly traded his curly fry recipe to a traveling salesman in exchange for the Guberburger recipe (which is funny because it's not much of a recipe at all). The Wheel Inn used to sell a smashed classic burger with a dollop of hot peanut butter, or "goober" as it was affectionately known.

But all of this came to a screeching halt when the Wheel Inn closed its doors in 2007. The classic drive-in, with carhop service until the end, met its demise for the very reason it existed—cars. The Wheel Inn was torn down, a victim of road widening at the busy corner on which it sat. Judy Clark, a longtime waitress (of forty-seven years!) bought the business and managed to reopen, only to close again for good a few years later.

The Wheel Inn was one of the original eight burger joints featured in my documentary film *Hamburger America*. When the audience saw peanut butter going on a burger for the first time they let out a collective moan—the condiment seemed implausible. The Guberburger wins converts though, usually the ones with an open mind who are unafraid of complex flavors. Anyone who has eaten Thai food and other tasty treats from Southeast Asia knows that the peanut plays a vital role in the cuisine. Beef satay, grilled beef on skewers accompanied by a peanut dipping sauce, is not far from the experience of the Guberburger.

765

Wheel Inn Drive-In, Sedalia, Missouri, 1947

For sixty years at the Wheel Inn the burger to order came standard with lettuce, tomato, and a smear of warmed peanut butter. I had a hard time cozying up to this burger at first, though it wasn't the peanut butter that turned me off. It was the strange addition of the salad items, and I took issue with the textures at play. From that point on I only ever ate Guber-burgers minus the lettuce and tomato. At most of the *Hamburger America* screenings we would serve Guberburgers, without lettuce and tomato. Then one day a friend (and a photographer for this book), Kris Brearton, told me he likes to put pickles on his version of the Guberburger. We tested it, and now I can't eat a Guberburger any other way.

THE GUBERBURGER

MAKES 8 BURGERS

EQUIPMENT

A cast-iron skillet or flat top

A large mixing bowl

A #12 salad scoop

A stiff spatula

A small saucepan

THE BURGER

Beef tallow (rendered beef fat; see
    page 18)

2 pounds (about 1 kg) fresh-ground
    80/20 chuck

Salt, for seasoning

1 cup (240 ml) creamy peanut butter

8 soft white buns, toasted (see instruc-
    tions, page 33)

THE TOPPINGS

Dill pickle chips

1 Preheat the cast-iron skillet over medium heat (or a flat top to medium) and add some beef tallow. Use the spatula to spread the fat, coating the cooking surface.

2 Place the ground beef in a mixing bowl and, using the salad scoop, form balls of beef, placing them on the heated skillet as you go. Each ball should have about 3 inches (7 cm) of space around it. (You may only be able to cook 2 or 3 burgers at a time.)

3 Add a generous pinch of salt to each ball of beef and then, using the stiff spatula, press them down *hard* until they become wide patties just a bit larger than the buns. Let them cook, undisturbed, for 2½ minutes or until reddish liquid begins to form on the surface of the patties.

4 As soon as the patties are smashed, heat the peanut butter in the small saucepan over low heat.

5 When they're ready, flip each patty *once* and don't press them again. Spoon some of the warm peanut butter over the patties and cook for another 2 minutes or so.

6 Meanwhile, add 2 or 3 pickle chips to each bottom bun and set aside.

7 When the patties are cooked through, remove them from the heat and place them on the prepared toasted buns. Serve with pride.

REGIONAL
FAVORITES

THE
WEST

CALIFORNIA

THE CLASSIC PATTY MELT

In the original version of this book, I included a recipe for a patty melt that was a combination of one from my youth and the classic version from California. It was disingenuous to refer to that burger as a "patty melt," and I'm here to correct my mistake. The elements that make up the classic patty melt should not suffer the fate of poetic license. There is only one way to make this burger and proudly call it a patty melt. As is so often the case, we look to history and we end up in Los Angeles.

The invention of the classic Southern California patty melt has been credited to William Wallace "Tiny" Naylor, who opened a very successful drive-in restaurant on Sunset Boulevard at La Brea. Open from 1949 to 1984, it was popular with celebrities because of its space-aged design and because they could eat without getting out of their cars. Fans of the Beastie Boys may recognize the drive-in from the vintage 1964 *Esquire* magazine photo on the cover of their album *Ill Communication*. According to legend, it was at Tiny Naylor's sometime in the 1950s that the famous patty melt was invented. There is some confusion in burger history that credits LA's Du-par's with the invention. There may be some truth here, because in 2004 Biff Naylor (Tiny's son) purchased Dupar's, and his daughter Jennifer introduced it to the revamped menu.

To stay completely authentic there are only four ingredients in a classic patty melt: a griddled beef patty, Swiss cheese, seeded rye bread, and

Tiny Naylor's Drive-In, Los Angeles, California, 1948

caramelized onions. Alter just one of these elements and you have slipped away from the proper definition. Full disclosure, the patty melt variation I put in my old book lives on (and is slightly bastardized as well) on page 224 as the Chester-Rouer.

THE CLASSIC PATTY MELT

MAKES 4 PATTY MELTS

EQUIPMENT

8 (8-inch/20-cm) parchment paper
    squares
2 seasoned cast-iron skillets
2 spatulas or turners

THE MELT

1 pound (about 500 g) fresh-ground
    80/20 chuck
Kosher salt
Butter
8 slices seeded rye bread
8 slices Swiss cheese
Caramelized Onions (see recipe,
    page 54)

1 Divide the beef into 4 equal portions (4 ounces/125 g) each.

2 Then, using 2 squares of parchment paper, hand-smash each portion between the sheets until they are about ⅛ inch (3 mm) thick.

3 Butter one side of each slice of bread and set aside.

4 Heat one skillet over medium-low heat and add as many pairs of bread slices as will fit comfortably, butter side down (you will likely have to do this in batches). Place a slice of cheese on top of each bread slice.

5 Heat the other skillet over medium-high heat and, when it is starting to smoke, add 2 of the patties. Add a pinch of salt to each patty in the pan and cook for about 3 minutes. Flip and cook for another minute, and transfer the cooked patties as they finish to the breads (one patty for each pair of bread slices). Then repeat with the other 2 patties.

6 Scoop a generous heap of the caramelized onions onto each patty, then flip the bread slice with cheese only on top of the patty (hopefully, at this point the cheese has melted a bit).

7 After a minute or so, use 2 spatulas to carefully flip the patty melts over in the pan. They should be golden brown and cooked perfectly. If not, keep flipping until both sides look amazing.

CALIFORNIA

THE BACON-AVOCADO TOAST BURGER

Although they are both savory, bacon and avocado are diametrically opposed ingredients. Avocados are a fruit (yep, not a vegetable) with extraordinary health benefits. They are *loaded* with vitamins and are said to help lower bad (LDL) cholesterol levels and raise good cholesterol (HDL). Bacon is, well, bacon. Its only health advantage is that consuming it makes you happy (and happiness is good for your health). The two together make for atypical bedfellows, but when combined on a burger, the result is magical.

The California connection to the avocado makes sense. The fruit has roots in Puebla, Mexico, but today California grows nearly every American avocado consumed. Also, the large Mexican population of Southern California most likely helped to put the avocado on menus throughout Los Angeles. It was only natural that slices of the buttery fruit would eventually find their way onto a burger patty. Places like Howard's Famous Bacon & Avocado Burgers, Astro Burgers in West Hollywood, and many others have been selling the burger for decades, and recently, the avocado-bacon combination has found its way onto menus at the Whataburger chain in Texas and as far away as fast-food menus in Japan.

I've recently discovered avocado toast thanks to its rise in popularity. It's one of the simplest healthy snacks you can whip up, and it involves only

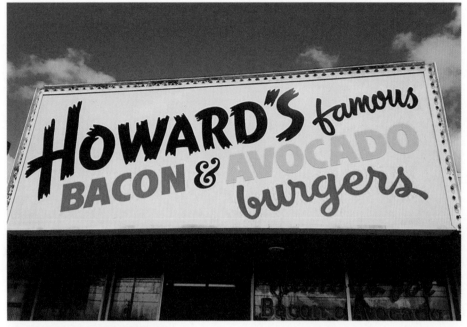

Howard's Famous, Los Angeles, California

five ingredients: toast, avocado, salt, olive oil, and paprika. I tried combining this treat with bacon and a burger patty, and the outcome was as predicted—incredible.

One of the biggest mistakes people make when constructing a burger that involves avocado is to add standard ingredients, such as lettuce, tomato, and pickle. And some of the most unnecessary ingredients to include are cheese and special sauces. Avocado is naturally creamy, so adding cheese becomes excessive. Embrace the integrity of these sparse ingredients and you'll agree that less is definitely more.

THE BACON-AVOCADO TOAST BURGER

MAKES 4 BURGERS

EQUIPMENT

A sharp paring knife

A seasoned cast-iron skillet

A stiff spatula

A medium-size mixing bowl

A #12 salad scoop

THE TOPPINGS

3 ripe avocados

Smoked paprika

Sea salt, to taste

8 slices cooked bacon (instructions on page 294)

THE BURGER

8 slices crusty bakery bread

Beef tallow (rendered beef fat; see page 18)

2 pounds (about 1 kg) fresh-ground 80/20 chuck

Salt, for seasoning

1 First, prepare the avocado toast. Lightly toast the bread slices in a toaster. Cut the avocados in half and remove the pits. Using a sharp paring knife, slice the flesh directly in the avocado shell and spoon out the contents.

2 Using a fork, mash the avocado a bit and press some onto each piece of toast, dividing it evenly. Sprinkle with paprika and salt to taste. Set aside.

3 Next, make the burgers according to the instructions for the Thick Pub Classic Burger on page 44. Preheat the cast-iron skillet over medium heat and add some beef tallow. Use the spatula to spread the fat, coating the cooking surface.

4 Add the cooked patties to the waiting avocado toasts and place the bacon on top.

5 Consume immediately, knowing that between the avocado and the bacon the healthy attributes are a wash (sort of).

HAWAII

THE LOCO MOCO

The next time you're in Hawaii, make a point of getting away from the mega-hotels and tourist traps to indulge in some true local fare. The cuisine of Hawaii is varied but heavily influenced by Japanese cooking and mainland American cuisine. You may be surprised to learn that Spam is a menu staple in most local cafes. As the story goes, Spam was the only meat product available to U.S. troops stationed in Hawaii during World War II. After the war the troops left and Spam remained.

Two unique variations on the burger in Hawaii are the Loco Moco and the teriyaki burger, both available at many cafes, counters, and restaurants throughout the Islands. Sure, you can visit a burger shop and get a ring of pineapple on a burger, but that's actually not authentically Hawaiian. In fact, the idea of ham and pineapple on a burger was created in Ontario, Canada, in the early 1960s, not in the Hawaiian Islands.

The Loco Moco has its roots in Hilo, Hawaii, specifically at the now-defunct Lincoln Grill. It was created in 1949 at the request of local high school football players, which makes sense looking at the ingredients. I lived on Maui for a while and had my share of local meals, mostly consisting of oxtail or Spam soup and beef chili over rice. I always marveled at the way Hawaiians put everything on rice, including burgers. The classic Loco Moco consists of a bed of white rice under a burger patty smothered in beef gravy, all topped with a fried egg. It is a sight to behold and equally tasty. Variations exist with Spam, beef chili, and fish. You should experiment, but here is my recipe for the classic—a good place to start.

THE LOCO MOCO

MAKES 4 SERVINGS

EQUIPMENT

A mandoline slicer

A seasoned cast-iron skillet

A stiff spatula

A medium-size mixing bowl

A #12 salad scoop

A small nonstick skillet

THE BURGER

Beef tallow (rendered beef fat; see
    page 18)

1 pound (about 500 g) fresh-ground
    80/20 chuck

1 medium Vidalia or Walla Walla onion,
    sliced into super-thin rings (translu-
    cent and thinner than paper)

Salt, for seasoning

2 cups (about 400 g) cooked white
    rice, prepared according to package
    directions

THE TOPPINGS

Super-Easy Tasty Brown Gravy (recipe
    follows)

4 large eggs

1 Make the brown gravy according to
recipe instructions (see opposite page).
Set aside.

2 Preheat the cast-iron skillet over medium heat, add some beef tallow, and use
the spatula to coat the cooking surface.

3 Place the ground beef in your mixing
bowl. Using the scoop, form heaping balls
of beef, gently releasing them into the hot
pan. Leave about 3 inches (7 cm) of space
surrounding each. (You may only be able to
cook 2 or 3 burgers at a time.)

4 Sprinkle a generous pinch of salt on each
ball of beef. Then grab a golf ball–size pile
of the thin-sliced onion and push it onto the
center of each ball of beef so it sticks.

5 With great force, use the stiff spatula to
press directly down onto the balls of beef,
smashing them into thin, wide patties.
The onions should fuse nicely with the raw
beef. Once they're smashed, don't touch the
patties again until they're ready to flip—
5 minutes or until red moisture begins to
form on the top of the patties.

6 While the burgers cook, pile ¼ cup
(50 g) of warm rice in each of four
single-serving bowls or on plates.

7 When red moisture begins to form on the patties, flip them and cook an additional 2 to 2½ minutes.

8 Meanwhile, in a clean, nonstick skillet, fry the eggs, sunny-side up or over-easy. You'll want the yolks to be runny because when the egg yolk meets the gravy, beef juice, and rice all hell will break loose on your taste buds (in a good way).

9 Place a cooked burger patty on each bed of rice, smother with the brown gravy, and top with a fried egg. Serve immediately.

SUPER-EASY TASTY BROWN GRAVY

Makes enough to smother 4 loco mocos

4 tablespoons (½ stick/55 g) butter
¼ cup (30 g) all-purpose flour
1 cup (240 ml) beef stock
½ teaspoon salt
¼ teaspoon black pepper
¼ teaspoon garlic powder
½ teaspoon Worcestershire sauce
2 tablespoons whole milk

1 Start by making a roux: Melt the butter in a small saucepan over low heat. Stir in the flour and whisk constantly until the mixture is browned and smells nutty, about 3 minutes. (Do not overcook!)

2 Slowly pour in the beef stock while whisking and reduce the heat and simmer. Keep stirring.

3 Add the salt, pepper, garlic powder, and Worcestershire sauce and continue to stir with the whisk.

4 Introduce the milk slowly, a little at a time, and keep stirring until creamy. Remove the pan from the heat. If your gravy gets too thick, stir in a bit more beef stock until you're happy with the consistency.

HAWAII

THE TERIYAKI BURGER

The teriyaki burger is as ubiquitous in Hawaii as the Loco Moco. My good friend Jennifer Binney, a Hawaii native who lives on Oahu, calls it the "old school diner burger," and she suggests serving it, "on the *whitest* white bun you can find. No seeds." Not surprisingly, the teriyaki burger has roots in Japan; it was invented by the MOS Burger chain in the early 1970s. Today in Japan it is everywhere. McDonald's even has a version of the teriyaki burger on the menu at their Japanese locations (so I've heard).

Depending on the *okazuya*, or local Hawaiian diner, where you are eating a "teri" burger, it could be marinated in teriyaki and cooked or it may have a thicker teriyaki sauce on top as a condiment. Some are simply marinated, like the burgers at the classic sixty-year-old W&M Bar-B-Q in Honolulu. The best ones use both teriyaki marinade and sauce, and a dollop of sweet Japanese mayonnaise to push the flavors over the edge. This burger screams umami.

THE TERIYAKI BURGER

MAKES 8 BURGERS

EQUIPMENT

A medium-size mixing bowl

A hand patty press set to make ⅜-inch (just over 1-cm) patties

Parchment paper, cut into 6-inch (15-cm) squares

A #12 salad scoop

A large casserole dish or baking pan

A seasoned cast-iron skillet

A stiff spatula

THE BURGER

Beef tallow (rendered beef fat; see page 18)

Teriyaki Marinade (recipe follows)

2 pounds (about 1 kg) fresh-ground 80/20 chuck

8 soft white buns, toasted (see instructions, page 33)

THE TOPPINGS

Japanese mayonnaise (preferably the ubiquitous Kewpie brand)

Iceberg lettuce, thinly shredded

1 medium Vidalia or Walla Walla onion, chopped

Teriyaki Sauce (recipe follows)

Important: Clean your cast-iron skillet immediately after you're done cooking these burgers.

1 Make the teriyaki marinade well in advance—it will take a while to cool adequately before it can be used.

2 Place the ground beef in the mixing bowl. Line a hand patty press with a square of parchment, and then, using the salad scoop, make a level ball of beef and place it in the center of the parchment. Place another square of parchment paper on top and press the lid of the patty press down hard.

3 Continue pressing patties until the meat is used up (you may have a little left over after pressing 8 patties).

4 Leaving the parchment paper on the patties, stack them on a plate and place them in the fridge until the marinade is cool or even chilled (if it isn't already).

5 Remove the patties from the fridge, remove the parchment paper, and place patties in a single layer in a large casserole dish. Cover with marinade and return to the fridge for at least 5 minutes. Note: If the marinade isn't cool enough, or if you leave the patties in the marinade for more than 30 minutes, the patties will fall apart in the sauce.

6 Preheat the cast-iron skillet over medium-low heat and add some beef tallow. The sugar content in the marinade will burn quickly at high heat, so be sure to keep the flame low.

7 Remove the marinated burgers from the fridge and lift them out of the marinade carefully with a spatula and onto the hot skillet. Let cook, untouched, for 5 to 5½ minutes or until red liquid begins to form on the surface of the patty.

8 While the burgers cook, line each toasted bottom bun with a squeeze of mayo, a pile of the shredded lettuce, and a bunch of chopped onions. Garnish each top bun with another squeeze of mayo. Set aside.

9 Flip the patties and cook for another 4 to 4½ minutes. When the patties are cooked through, transfer them to the toasted buns. Add a dollop of the teriyaki sauce followed by the top bun and serve.

TERIYAKI SAUCE
Makes more than enough to top 8 burgers

½ cup (120 ml) soy sauce
½ cup (120 ml) mirin (sweet rice wine)
¼ cup (55 g) packed brown sugar
4 cloves garlic, minced (may substitute 1 teaspoon garlic powder)
1 teaspoon grated fresh ginger (may substitute ½ teaspoon ground ginger)
1 tablespoon plus 2 teaspoons cornstarch

1 In a small saucepan, combine the soy sauce, mirin, brown sugar, ¾ cup (180 ml) water, garlic, and ginger, stir, and bring to a boil. Cover, reduce the heat to a simmer, and cook for 10 minutes.
2 Using a mesh sieve, strain out the garlic and ginger solids.
3 Return the sauce to the saucepan over medium-low heat and whisk in the cornstarch, stirring constantly until the sauce begins to thicken. Remove the pan from the heat and continue whisking until the sauce reaches a stable consistency.
4 Cover and set aside until ready to use.

TERIYAKI MARINADE
Makes enough to marinate 8 teriyaki burgers

¼ cup (60 ml) soy sauce
¼ cup (60 ml) mirin (sweet rice wine)
2 tablespoons packed brown sugar
2 cloves garlic, minced (may substitute ½ teaspoon garlic powder)
½ teaspoon finely chopped fresh ginger (may substitute ¼ teaspoon ground ginger)

1 In a medium saucepan, combine the soy sauce, mirin, brown sugar, 3 cups (720 ml) water, garlic, and ginger, stir, and bring to a boil. Cover, reduce the heat and simmer, and cook for 10 minutes.
2 Remove from the heat and allow the marinade to cool thoroughly before pouring it over the beef patties. (You can stick the saucepan in the freezer for a few minutes to accelerate cooling.)

Note: If you don't want chunks of garlic and ginger in your marinade, transfer the cooked sauce to a blender and then remove the solids using a mesh sieve.

MONTANA

THE NUTBURGER

When I first got wind of this burger, I planned a trip out West to Matt's Place in Butte, Montana, almost immediately. Burgers with nuts (like the Guberburger of Missouri and the Cashew Burger at Anchor Bar in Superior, Wisconsin) have always piqued my interest, and the Nutburger was no exception. And much like the Guber and Cashew burgers, this one is hard to get to, leaving me with the impression that burgers involving nuts are only for those with a serious case of wanderlust. In other words, unless you are a local, the Nutburger is a destination burger.

In the late 1930s, Matt Korn traveled to Southern California and ate a burger with peanuts and mayonnaise. Matt was so taken by the burger that he returned to Butte, opened Matt's Place Drive-In, and featured the Nutburger on the menu. Today, the original structure still stands and is one of the only burger joints on the National Register of Historic Places (Louis' Lunch, the possible birthplace of the hamburger, is another). And as far as I know, Matt's is one of the only places that still serves a Nutburger.

Nuts work so well on a burger because they are salty and contain tasty oils. What nuts add, in addition, is a texture that is unlike any other food out there. Bacon and crisp lettuce can contribute a nice crunchy texture to a hamburger, but it's hard to find anything to match the mouthfeel of nuts.

The concept is simple and there are no secrets here. When an order for a Nutburger comes in at Matt's, the counterperson takes a spoonful of crushed peanuts out of the ice cream sundae bar and deposits them in a coffee mug. To that, a dollop of sweet Miracle Whip is stirred in, and the

Matt's Place Drive-In, Butte, Montana

concoction is immediately applied to one of Matt's tasty smashed classic patties. The Nutburger must be experienced to be appreciated.

Sadly, you won't be able to sample this burger at its birthplace in Montana—in 2018 Matt's closed its doors for good. Use the following recipe as the next best thing. Keep hamburger history alive and make yourself a few nutburgers.

THE NUTBURGER

MAKES 8 BURGERS

EQUIPMENT

A clean kitchen cloth

A mallet or meat tenderizer or a rolling pin for crushing the peanuts

A small- and a medium-size mixing bowl

A seasoned cast-iron skillet

A stiff spatula

A #12 salad scoop

THE TOPPINGS

1 cup (150 g) roasted, salted peanuts (without shells or skins)

½ cup (120 ml) Miracle Whip (see Note)

THE BURGER

Beef tallow (rendered beef; see page 18)

2 pounds (about 1 kg) fresh-ground 80/20 chuck

Salt, for seasoning

8 soft white buns, toasted (see instructions, page 33)

Note: The flavor of Miracle Whip can be achieved with ½ cup (120 ml) mayonnaise mixed with 2 teaspoons sugar and a dash of paprika and onion powder.

1 Shortly before you cook the burgers, crush the peanuts by laying them out on a cutting board or butcher block and covering them with a clean kitchen cloth. Smash with a mallet or rolling pin until the peanuts are crumbled (if you've made a powder, you've gone too far).

2 Mix the crushed peanuts with the Miracle Whip (or substitute) in the small mixing bowl until combined. The topping should have a relatively thick consistency. Set aside.

3 Preheat the cast-iron skillet over medium heat and add some beef tallow to coat the surface.

4 Place the ground chuck in the medium mixing bowl and use the salad scoop to make balls of beef, placing them in the skillet as you go. Each ball should have about 3 inches (7 cm) of space around it. (You may only be able to cook 2 or 3 burgers at a time.)

5 Add a generous pinch of salt to each ball of beef and, using the stiff spatula, press them down hard. Once flat, don't touch them again. Let cook for 2½ minutes or until reddish liquid begins to form on the surface of the patties.

6 Flip them *once*, and resist the temptation to press them again. Cook for another 2 minutes or until cooked through.

7 Transfer the patties to the toasted buns and top with a heaping spoonful of the peanut condiment followed by the top bun. Serve immediately.

NEW MEXICO

THE GREEN CHILE CHEESEBURGER

The New Mexican chile graces nearly every single menu in the state and is rarely found elsewhere. It is a defining aspect of New Mexican cooking and is served either green or red. Green chile has a subtle, earthy flavor, whereas red chile (left on the vine to ripen after the initial fall harvest) has a deep, smoky essence. Both can be found hot or mild, but the best New Mexican chile falls right in the middle, where you can feel some heat and still taste that chile. It's one of the most distinctive natural flavors in America.

But green chile is not native to New Mexico. The story of how the pepper found its way to the region is fascinating, and begins with Christopher Columbus's second journey to the Caribbean in the late fifteenth century. He returned to Spain with seeds, introducing Europe to a spicy pepper for the first time. Fifty years later, as Spanish conquistadors colonized the Southwest, they brought their peppers along, altering the area's generally bland diet forever.

Unless you've had the great fortune to taste this pepper firsthand it's somewhat difficult to describe. Imagine a mild Anaheim pepper (a close relative) crossed with a spicy jalapeño—but even that's not accurate. Most New Mexicans roast their chiles over an open flame to enable easy removal of the skin, leaving the flesh of the pepper soft and smoky. Add this, chopped and stewed, to a thick cheeseburger and prepare your mouth for an out-of-body experience. Every single person I have ever introduced to the Green Chile

Cheeseburger has gratified me with an ear-to-ear smile following their first bite.

Hit up a touristy spot in New Mexico and, most likely, green chile will be served mild on your burger. Head to the locals' favorite spots for real-deal heat. It's never too hot, but usually served just spicy enough to give you a little endorphin buzz. Writer John T. Edge once described the sensation as how you might feel after shotgunning two beers in rapid succession. He's not far off.

By design, there's not much to a great green chile cheeseburger, except, of course, the right chile. Many suppliers near Hatch, New Mexico, will ship you fresh green chiles that you can roast, peel, and eat, but the season is brief (September). New Mexicans are big on freezing chopped chile, making it available by mail all year long. And as for condiments, they are not necessary here. Keep things simple so that you can taste the unadulterated beauty of green chile and beef. Use a good, sharp melty cheddar to glue the whole thing together.

THE GREEN CHILE CHEESEBURGER

MAKES 6 CHEESEBURGERS

EQUIPMENT

A small saucepan

A 3½-inch (9-cm) food ring or round cutter (recommended, but not required)

Parchment paper

A seasoned cast-iron skillet or flat top

2 or 3 medium-size metal bowls

THE BURGER

3 cups (450 g) roasted, peeled, and chopped New Mexican green chiles

Splash of water or beef stock

2 pounds (about 1 kg) fresh-ground 80/20 chuck

Beef tallow (rendered beef fat; see page 18)

Salt and black pepper for seasoning

White cheddar cheese, sliced

6 seeded soft white buns, toasted (see instructions, page 33)

THE TOPPINGS

Don't even think about it. Toppings other than chile and cheese are completely unnecessary.

1 Add the green chiles to the small sauce-pan with a splash of water or beef stock (just enough to let the chiles steam slightly, but not so much it turns into soup). Cover and heat over medium heat until hot. Remove from the heat, keep covered, and set aside.

2 Divide the beef into 6 even portions (a little over 5½ ounces/155 g each).

3 Line a clean surface or cutting board with parchment paper to prevent stick-ing. Working with the food ring, gently press one portion of the beef into the ring to create a perfectly round patty. Don't over-press—you want it to maintain a somewhat loose grind. Repeat with the remaining beef.

4 Add some beef tallow to the cast-iron skillet, using the spatula to spread the fat, and crank it up to medium-high heat. When the pan just starts to smoke, it's ready.

5 At this point, and not before, season both sides of the patties with a liberal amount of salt and pepper. Salting too early will bind the muscle fibers together and make the burgers tough (not good).

6 Place the patties in the hot skillet—the beef should sizzle loudly when it hits the pan—and cook for 4 minutes without dis-turbing them. The goal here is to sear your burgers, sealing in the juices. When you see red liquid start to form on the top of the patties, it's time to flip them.

7 Reduce the heat to medium and cook the second side of the patties (without disturb-ing them) for an additional 6½ minutes. After 4 minutes, add a healthy pile of the green chiles to the top of each patty fol-lowed by a slice of cheese. To help melt the cheese, cover the burgers with a metal bowl or large pot lid for the final 2 to 3 minutes of cooking.

8 Remove the skillet from the heat and allow the burgers to rest for 1½ minutes. The internal temperature of the burgers should be about 143°F (62°C) for medium-rare. Transfer to the toasted buns with nothing else. Serve immediately.

NEW MEXICO
THE TORTILLA BURGER

Red or green? It's the state question of New Mexico. If someone asks you this, you are probably placing an order for something very tasty.

The New Mexican chile, a staple of the state's diet, is available in red or green (see page 130). The red color is the result after a green chile has stayed on the vine for an additional four to five weeks to ripen. But unlike green chile (which is generally found fresh-roasted and diced) red chile is normally found in powdered form and used for seasoning and sauces. Many take great pride in making the best possible red chile sauce.

Like chile Colorado sauce, the red sauce found on just about all Tex-Mex food throughout the Southwest, red chile sauce is made from grinding oven- or sun-dried red chile pods and mixing them with a few very basic ingredients. Chile Colorado tends to be more complex and spicy, whereas red chile sauce is all about the simple, smoky flavor of the pepper, with less emphasis on the heat (though red chile sauce can be super hot). The sauce is not something you dip food into—in New Mexico foods like breakfast burritos, enchiladas, and tacos are literally swimming in a deep pool of the stuff. It was only a matter of time before someone decided to take a burger for a swim in it, too.

In New Mexico there are a few great examples of the tortilla burger, which was said to have been invented at Maria's Restaurant in Santa Fe in the 1950s. One of my favorites can be found at the beloved, decades-old Santa Fe diner The Pantry (just down the street from Maria's). Its basic construction is almost a rule-breaker to me as it's more of a hamburger "dish"

599   284

The Pantry Restaurant, Santa Fe, New Mexico

than a sandwich. And like the Loco Moco of Hawaii (page 120), it's one of the only burgers in America I will eat with a knife and fork. There's just no other way to consume this beautiful expression of New Mexican ingenuity.

A griddle-cooked patty is added to a soft flour tortilla that has been prepped with refried beans and shredded cheddar cheese. The tortilla is then wrapped or folded and smothered with red chile sauce, covered with more shredded cheddar, and placed under a broiler to melt. I love this burger experience.

THE TORTILLA BURGER

MAKES 4 BURGERS

EQUIPMENT

Parchment paper

A 4½-inch (12-cm) food ring or round cutter

A large seasoned cast-iron skillet

A second large skillet to warm the tortillas

A stiff spatula

Ovenproof plates

THE BURGER

2 pounds (about 1 kg) fresh-ground 80/20 chuck

Beef tallow (rendered beef fat; see page 18)

Salt and black pepper

4 large flour tortillas (the ones used for sandwich wraps and burritos)

Frijoles Refritos de Jorge (refried beans; page 173)

8 ounces (225 g) sharp cheddar, shredded (reserve half for topping)

THE TOPPINGS

Basic Red Chile Sauce (recipe follows)

Shredded cheddar (reserved from above)

1 Divide the ground beef into 4 even portions (8 ounces/250 g each).

2 Line a clean work surface or cutting board with parchment paper to prevent sticking. Working with your food ring, gently press a portion of beef into the ring to create a perfectly round patty. Don't over-press the meat—you want it to maintain a somewhat loose grind. Repeat with the remaining beef.

3 Add some beef tallow to the cast-iron skillet, using the spatula to spread the fat, and crank it up to medium-high heat. When the pan just starts to smoke, it's ready.

4 At this point, and not before, season both sides of the patties with a liberal amount of salt (and pepper, if desired). Salting too early will bind the muscle fibers together and make your burgers tough (not good).

5 Place the patties in the hot skillet—the beef should sizzle loudly when it hits the pan—and cook for 5 minutes without disturbing them. The goal here is to sear the burgers, sealing in the juices. When you see red liquid start to form on the uncooked surface of the burger, it's time to flip them.

6 Reduce the heat to medium and cook the second side, without disturbing them, for an additional 5 minutes.

7 While the burgers are cooking, warm the tortillas in the other (dry) skillet for 1 minute on each side.

8 Remove the burgers from the heat and allow them to rest for 1½ minutes. The internal temperature of the burgers should be about 143°F (62°C) for medium-rare.

9 While the burgers are resting, add a smear of the refried beans to the center of each warm tortilla. Top the beans with a handful of the shredded cheese, followed by the cooked patty. Fold the edges of the tortilla up around the burger and flip it over, placing the folded side down on the plate. Repeat with the rest of the tortillas, beans, half of the cheese, and the burgers.

9 Ladle enough chile sauce over each tortilla-wrapped burger to smother it, and add another handful of the reserved shredded cheese to each.

10 Place each plate under a broiler until the cheese melts. Remove, and serve immediately. You are welcome.

BASIC RED CHILE SAUCE
Makes enough to smother 4 tortilla burgers

To make this sauce you will need to get your hands on some good dried red chile powder from New Mexico. It's available everywhere in the state, can be mail-ordered, and is not expensive. You can substitute other ground red chile, but for the real-deal go New Mexican. I use mild red chile because sometimes New Mexican red chile can be very hot. You can always add heat later (with hot sauce).

A glug of olive oil
2 cloves garlic
2 cups (480 ml) chicken stock or water
½ cup (48 g) mild dried red chile powder, preferably from New Mexico
1 teaspoon ground cumin
Sea salt, to taste

1 In a large saucepan, heat the oil over medium heat and add the garlic. Cook for about a minute or until just golden brown.
2 Add the chicken stock and red chile, cover, and simmer for 15 minutes.
3 Transfer to a blender and blend until smooth.
4 Return the red chile sauce to the saucepan and season with the cumin and salt. Cover and simmer the sauce for an additional 30 minutes. Keep covered and warm while you make the burgers.

UTAH

THE PASTRAMI BURGER

It was not predestined that this burger would become a regional specialty of Utah. But like just about everything else in life, there's a perfectly good explanation for this unlikely occurrence. It started with the Greeks, of course.

There are so many stories about Greeks in the burger business that it would take an entire book to track their remarkable achievements in American burger history. The Billy Goat in Chicago; South 21 Drive-In in Charlotte, North Carolina; Zaharakos in Columbus, Indiana; and Val's Burgers in Hayward, California, are just a few Greek-American burger success stories. So it's not surprising to me that the pastrami burger was the result of a Greek burgerman, namely James Katsanevas.

Katsanevas opened Minos Burgers in Anaheim, California, in the early 1970s and served a pastrami burger, but he was not the first. By the mid-twentieth century, Jews who had left New York City for life in the West brought a favorite comfort food with them, and soon pastrami stands and counters dotted Los Angeles. When Southern California's burger culture met the cured, smoked pastrami imported from the East Coast, it was a match made in burger heaven. Many of the stands that served pastrami burgers are gone, but a few remain, like Johnny's Pastrami and George's Burger Stand in Los Angeles (Greek-owned) and the Hat in Alhambra.

In the early 1980s, Katsanevas moved to Salt Lake City and brought the pastrami burger with him. He had family in the nightclub business there, and by 1982 the delicacy was on the menu at the Katsanevases' new venture,

The Hat, Alhambra, California, 1950s

Crown Burgers. Today, many pastrami burgers can be found all over Salt Lake City, but some of the best are at Crown.

A cheeseburger bursting with a soft pile of glorious pastrami is a sight to behold. Add some Classic Utah Fry Sauce (page 145) and you have one helluva flavor bomb. Fry sauce is a very basic condiment, usually made from equal amounts of ketchup and mayonnaise. But if you're at Crown Burger, expect something a bit different. Owner Mike Katsanevas once told me, "We make our fry sauce in house with seven ingredients; most of them secret."

THE PASTRAMI BURGER

MAKES 8 BURGERS

EQUIPMENT

A seasoned cast-iron skillet or flat top

A medium-size mixing bowl

A #12 salad scoop

A stiff spatula

THE BURGER

8 seeded soft white buns, toasted
    (see instructions, page 33)

Beef tallow (rendered beef fat; see
    page 18)

2 pounds (about 1 kg) fresh-ground
    80/20 chuck

Salt, for seasoning

8 slices American cheese

THE TOPPINGS

Fry Sauce (recipe follows)

1 medium Vidalia or Walla Walla onion,
    sliced

Iceberg lettuce, shredded

1 pound (about 500 g) of the best
    deli pastrami you can find, sliced
    super-thin

1 Make the fry sauce according to instructions. Top the bottoms of each toasted bun with a dollop of fry sauce followed by onion slices and shredded lettuce. Set aside.

2 Preheat the cast-iron skillet over medium (or a flat top to medium) and add some beef tallow. Use the spatula to spread the fat, coating the surface.

3 Place the ground chuck in the mixing bowl and use the salad scoop to make balls of beef, placing them on the heated skillet as you go. Each ball should have about 3 inches (7 cm) of space around it. Depending on the size of your cooking surface, you may only be able to cook 2 or 3 burgers at a time.

4 Sprinkle a generous pinch of salt on each ball of beef and then, using your stiff spatula, press them down, hard. Don't be afraid, press harder! Press that ball until it's a wide patty just a bit larger than the bun it's about to meet. Once the burgers are flat, let them cook for 2½ minutes or until reddish liquid begins to form on the surface of the patties.

5 Flip them *once*, and resist the temptation to press the patties again. Add a slice of cheese to each patty and let them sit for another 2 minutes or until cooked through.

6 Now is a good time to warm up the pastrami. Place it in a covered microwave-safe dish and cook in the microwave on high for 1 minute. (Or, for best results, place the pastrami in a bowl inside a covered stovetop steamer for a few minutes until warm.)

7 Using the spatula, remove the burgers from the skillet and place them on the prepared buns, on top of the lettuce. Next add a heaping pile of the thin-sliced pastrami (bunch it up—don't lay it flat on the patties). Add another dollop of fry sauce to the inside of the top buns, sandwich them, and enjoy. These will make a bacon cheeseburger seem downright silly.

CLASSIC UTAH FRY SAUCE
**Makes enough to
top 8 pastrami burgers**

½ cup (120 ml) ketchup (or swap in barbecue sauce for fun)
½ cup (120 ml) mayonnaise
2 teaspoons sweet relish
Dash of onion powder

In a small bowl, mix all of the ingredients until well combined. Use on burgers and as a dip for fries, too.

REGIONAL
FAVORITES

THE
SOUTH

OKLAHOMA

THE THETA SPECIAL

Many people outside of Oklahoma consider the El Reno fried onion burger to be the state's official burger. But Oklahoma is home to a few iconic specialties (I'm thinking of the Seismic Burger from Meers Store and the Caesar Burger from the defunct Split-T in Oklahoma City, among others). And then there is the pride of Central Oklahoma, the eighty-five-year-old Theta burger.

The beloved burger was invented by Ralph Geist in 1937 at his bar Town Tavern, in Norman, Oklahoma. The bar was very close to the Oklahoma University campus, and apparently Ralph had grown tired of fielding the myriad late-night requests from the Kappa Alpha Theta sorority. Together, the girls and Ralph designed the now iconic burger and named it the Theta Special. Town Tavern is long gone, but the Theta can still be found at burger joints throughout the state. Johnnie's in Oklahoma City today makes one of the finest examples.

The key to a great Theta burger is a hickory sauce that may be more famous than the burger itself. The story spans over fifty years, involves a few Ralphs, four states, and a restaurant named Goody Goody. It's too much to explain here, but let's just say that in the lexicon of burger sauces, this one is a primary-source sauce that needs to be appreciated. At one point early on it was called "comeback sauce" (not the mayo-based comeback people refer to today), but Ralph renamed it hickory sauce when he opened Town Tavern (even though the recipe was a gift from the creator of the sauce).

Split-T, Oklahoma City, Oklahoma, 1993

The sauce on a Theta burger is basically a sweet barbecue sauce. Many versions of an "original" recipe exist online, but if you are using a classic hickory smoke barbecue sauce you are almost there. Johnnie's and the beloved (defunct) Split-T both sell and deliver their own Theta sauce by the jar if you want to create historically accurate Theta burgers.

There are only six elements to a Theta burger. If you get these six elements correct, your taste buds will soar. There is talk that Johnnie's uses shredded American cheese, but a mild, soft cheddar will do the trick. And to truly call it a Theta, you MUST charbroil the patties for that flame-licked backyard flavor. You should end up with a burger that is a pure velvety mélange of tang, smoke, and beef.

THE THETA SPECIAL

MAKES 5 BURGERS

EQUIPMENT

A charcoal grill

A long-handled grill spatula/turner

6 (8-inch/20-cm) parchment paper
   squares

A #12 (green) scoop

THE BURGER

1 pound (about 500 g) fresh ground
   80/20 chuck

5 seeded soft buns, toasted (see
   page 33)

Hickory smoke barbecue sauce

Shredded mild cheddar cheese (or a
   block of American cheese)

Dill pickle chips

Mayonnaise

1 Scoop the beef into 5 balls and hand-smash between 2 sheets of parchment (peel top layer off and reuse for the next 4, stacking the patties as you go).

2 Put your patties in the fridge while you heat the grill and prep your toppings.

3 Get your coals good and hot and prepare all your other ingredients to have them ready (including your toasted buns) because this is going to happen *fast*.

4 With your charcoal grill open, place all 5 patties on the grill grate and watch the magic unfold. Unlike grilled thick patties, where it's best to cover the grill for a portion of the cooking, here you want an open flame and super-fast cook times. Keep an eye on the patties, as they may be ready to flip in just 1 minute, depending on the temperature of your coals. If there are flames rising up and consuming the patties, you are doing the right thing.

5 Flip and cook for another minute or so.

6 Using your long-handled spatula, transfer the patties to your waiting buns. Top each patty with a good-sized dollop of the barbecue sauce, then a handful of the shredded cheese, followed by a few pickle chips.

7 Swipe the inside of the bun crown with mayonnaise and you are done.

8 Now go make more; folks are already asking.

THE FRIED-ONION BURGER

Oklahoma is one of my favorite places to immerse myself in burger culture. It sits in the center of what I like to call the American Burger Belt, an invisible line that can be drawn from Texas north to Wisconsin. This is where the majority of America's primary-source hamburgers can be found; the burgers that are unaffected by time or trend. The ones that have been made the same way for, in some cases, a hundred years. One of those burgers is the fried-onion burger of Oklahoma.

El Reno, Oklahoma is the epicenter of the fried-onion burger universe. At one point there were more than nine joints in town that served this regional treat. Today only a handful of places remain, but they are preserving an important piece of American food history.

An entrepreneurial burger man named Ross Davis, at the long-gone Hamburger Inn, used a handful of thin-sliced onions in his burger, and a legend was born. El Reno was a railroad town, and the Railway Shopman's Strike of 1922 had a massive impact on every resident. Ross's idea allowed him to stretch his daily beef supply while accidentaly creating a very tasty burger. Sid's Diner, Robert's Grill, and Johnnie's Grill in El Reno are the greatest guardians of this unique hamburger tradition. They continue that legacy by taking a gob of onions and smashing it into a ball of beef on the flat top. The contents fuse, creating a beautiful, caramelized, onion-beef mess that tastes incredible. The griddle masters who smash hundreds of these burgers daily at lunch are not shy about the amount of sliced onion they use, and the onion-to-beef ratio at Sid's is close to 50/50.

Hamburger Inn, El Reno, Oklahoma

Similar to the Griddle-Smashed Classic Cheeseburger (page 32) this method goes against everything you've been taught about how to treat a burger on a cooking surface. Pressing the life out of a burger seems wrong until you try it. And there's no other way to make this burger.

The trick to retain the juiciness here is to press the patty only *once* at the beginning and allow the burger to cook in its own grease, a sort of burger confit, if you will.

THE FRIED-ONION BURGER

MAKES 8 BURGERS

EQUIPMENT

A large seasoned cast-iron skillet or flat top

A stiff spatula

A medium-size mixing bowl

A #12 salad scoop

A mandoline slicer, set to its thinnest setting (you can use a sharp knife, but it will be very hard to get the onions thin enough without a mandoline)

THE BURGER

Beef tallow (rendered beef fat; see page 18

2 pounds (about 1 kg) fresh-ground 80/20 chuck

Salt, for seasoning

2 large Vidalia onions, sliced super-thin (they should be translucent and thinner than paper)

American cheese, deli-sliced

8 soft white buns

THE TOPPINGS

Always serve with a few slices of dill pickle chips on the side.

1 Preheat the cast-iron skillet over medium heat (or a flat top to medium) and add some beef tallow. Spread the fat with the flat side of your spatula to coat the surface.

2 Place the ground beef in the mixing bowl. Using the salad scoop, form balls of beef, gently releasing them into the hot pan with 2 to 3 inches (5 to 7 cm) of space surrounding each. (You may only be able to cook 2 or 3 burgers at a time.)

3 Season each beef ball with salt. Grab a golf ball–size pile of the thin-sliced onion and push it into each ball of beef. You'll want the onions to fall around the ball, not just be piled on top.

4 Smash each ball to make a patty. This requires more force than you'd think. Don't worry about smashing the patties too thin—they'll shrink to the size of your buns as they cook. Once they're smashed, don't touch again until ready to flip—just a few minutes, or until red moisture begins to form on the tops of the patties.

5 Flip the glorious beef-and-onion-fused patties and tuck some stray onions underneath. Slide a slice of American cheese on top of each, then add the bun. There is a tried-and-true method here I call "letting it ride": Atop the cheese, place the crown of the bun, cut side down. Then the heel, cut side down, on top of that. The beef steam will soften your buns. Cook for an additional 3 to 4 minutes, then carefully lift up the burger and buns with the spatula. Take the heel and place cut side up underneath the spatula blade, and in one swift move pinch and pull the burger off. Serve immediately.

THE SMOKED BURGER

When most people think of smoked meats, brisket, pork ribs, and bacon come to mind. It's the tougher cuts of meat that get the slow-and-low treatment, simply because cooking at lower temperatures with smoke helps to render fat, add flavor, and break down their muscle fibers. The beef that goes into your burger comes from a part of the cow that needs very little cooking—so good that it can be eaten raw (speak to your butcher before attempting this stunt). So why would you take a good cut of meat and smoke it? For the flavor.

There's no denying the irresistible quality of smoke when applied to food. There's something truly primordial about smoking meat that unlocks an ancient instinct in our brains. Most people who know how to cook with smoke would scoff at the idea of a burger being cooked for longer than 5 minutes or by any other method other than over a direct heat source. It's time to put aside preconceived notions of what should and should not be smoked and go smoke yourself a burger.

The first time I came across a smoked burger was, not surprisingly, in Texas. Good friend and food scribe Robb Walsh told me about a butcher in Houston who was selling a limited number of burgers a day that he was tossing in a Southern Pride electric rotisserie smoker designed to hold racks of ribs. The idea sounded absurd to me, but these guys would sell out of all two hundred burgers by the end of lunch. Robb explained to me that most people were getting the toppings all wrong by asking for a standard lettuce, tomato, onion combination. The key was to ask for barbecue sauce, pickles,

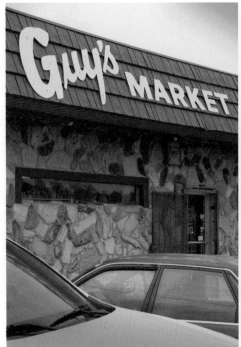

and raw onion. This, of course, turned out to be the right move. The tangy barbecue sauce perfectly complements the deeply infused smoke essence. Barbecue is a place where lettuce does not belong.

I will smoke anything, literally. My menu at the smoker is never limited to brisket alone. Chicken, salmon, and oysters do well in my smoker; even olives are amazing smoked if you have the room (recipe follows, page 161). And if you call yourself a competent pit master, it's only natural that you should find a place in your smoker for a few burger patties.

THE SMOKED BURGER

MAKES 5 BURGERS

EQUIPMENT

A kettle grill with a built-in lid thermometer and a hinged smoking grate

A bag of hardwood smoking chips (hickory, cherry, etc.)

Charcoal briquettes or lump charcoal

A charcoal chimney for igniting the charcoal

Long tongs (skip the plastic tips!)

THE BURGER

2 pounds (about 1 kg) fresh-ground 80/20 chuck

Salt, for seasoning

5 soft white buns or potato rolls, toasted (see instructions, page 33)

THE TOPPINGS

Dill pickle chips

Homemade BBQ Sauce (recipe follows)

1 or 2 Vidalia or Walla Walla onions, sliced and served raw or sautéed

1 Divide the meat into 5 portions and hand-form each portion into a 6-ounce (170-g) patty that's ¾ inch (2 cm) thick. Place in a covered container and refrigerate.

2 Prepare a smoker in the kettle grill, pushing the hot coals to one side of the grill. Position the hinged grate so you have access to the coals.

3 When the smoker is hot (around 225°F/110°C), salt both sides of the patties just before you place them inside the smoker (if you salt too early your burgers will stiffen).

4 Place the seasoned patties on the side of the grill rack opposite the coals (but not beyond the center of the grilling surface). Add a handful of the hickory chips to the hot coals and cover the grill immediately. Close down both the top and bottom vents slightly. Use these vents to control the temperature and limit airflow inside the kettle grill. You'll want to maintain a temperature near 225°F (110°C). If your smoke is running hotter than this, close the air louvers further to help find the proper temperature. Check the coals and condition of the chips every 15 minutes or so, but resist the temptation to open the grill lid too often—precious smoke will escape. If no smoke is present after 15 minutes, crack the vents, add more soaked wood chips, and put the lid back on.

5 Flip the patties after 25 minutes in the smoker, and smoke for an additional 25 to 30 minutes.

6 Place the smoked patties on toasted buns, and top with pickle chips, sliced or sautéed onion, and barbecue sauce. Serve immediately.

HOMEMADE BBQ SAUCE
Makes enough to
top 5 smoked burgers

2 tablespoons canola oil,
  or other neutral oil
3 cloves garlic, minced
1 cup (240 ml) ketchup
½ cup (120 ml) apple cider vinegar
¼ cup (60 ml) Worcestershire sauce
¼ cup (50 g) raw sugar or turbinado
3 tablespoons (45 ml) Steen's pure cane
  syrup or good-quality molasses
3 tablespoons (45 ml) bottled yellow
  mustard

1 Heat the oil in a saucepan and then add the garlic. Cook for about 2 minutes or until the garlic has just started to turn golden brown (do not burn).

2 Add the ketchup, vinegar, Worcestershire, sugar, cane syrup, and mustard. Stir to combine, cover, and let simmer for 30 minutes, stirring often. Store leftovers in a sealed container in the fridge for up to 2 weeks.

SMOKED OLIVES
Makes as many olives as
you have on hand

Every time I set up my charcoal grill to smoke burgers I feel guilty about wasting all of that unused smoke (smoked burgers take only about an hour). I thought of all the things I could smoke after the burgers are off the grill, and then I had an epiphany.

This method for smoking olives is ridiculously easy, especially if your smoker is already cranking. Make a bunch to wow your barbecue guests, or for a snack later on.

EQUIPMENT

A kettle grill set up for smoking (indirect heat with wet wood chips), or a smoker
Aluminum foil
Long tongs (skip the plastic tips!)

INGREDIENTS

A handful of good green olives with pits (Spanish or Colossal)

1 On a clean, flat surface, lay out a double layer of aluminum foil large enough to wrap up the amount of olives you intend to smoke.

2 Drain the olives and place them in the center of the foil. Fold the foil up and around the olives to create a basket shape with a folded seam on top.

3 Use a fork to poke several holes on all sides of the foil package.

4 Put the foil package in the smoker and smoke for about an hour. Use a grill mitt or long tongs to remove. These taste great hot off the grill but even better after they've cooled in the fridge for an hour. Will stay tasty up to a week refrigerated.

TEXAS

THE SWINE AND CHEESE

John T. Edge, friend and Southern food scribe, was the first to point me in the direction of the Squealer. "There's this place South of Houston," he told me years ago. "It's just a roadhouse, but they make *great* burgers. You should check it out, and they grind bacon *right into the patty*!" Indeed they did, and I wasted no time getting to that roadhouse. When I arrived at Tookie's Hamburgers I met my first bacon burger. My burger universe had been turned upside down.

Back then (more than a decade ago) grinding bacon into a hamburger patty was unheard of. These days it seems everyone is trying their hand at bacon burgers like the Squealer. I've recently seen them at restaurants in most major cities with names like the Piggie and the 50/50; even celebrated chef Sean Brock has his own very popular version.

The bacon burger embodies some of the greatest primordial flavors known to man: smoke, salt, beef, and bacon. It's rare that I would ever suggest mixing anything into good, fresh ground beef, but I will make an exception with bacon (which is great with anything, duh). When ground bacon and beef meet, something very special happens. It's a match made in heaven.

Tookie's suffered a tremendous blow and failed to reopen after Hurricane Ike devastated the Galveston, Texas, area in 2008. But it was sold and managed to reopen three years later, based on the tremendous popularity of the Squealer alone. I've been back since and am happy to report that

the burger rode out the storm, and actually grew in size and quality under new ownership.

The recipe for the Squealer is so secret that only a handful of people are aware of its contents. I've heard that competing restaurants have sent busboys down to Tookie's for jobs with the sole purpose of stealing the recipe. Apparently they never get the job. That said, this is *not* the Squealer recipe and I didn't try to get a job at Tookie's. It's a version we dubbed the Swine and Cheese. After much trial and error we created a version in the Hamburger America Test Kitchen that turned out dreamy. The greatest thing about this recipe is that you'll need to pull out your grinder and really get personal with your beef.

THE SWINE AND CHEESE

MAKES 4 LARGE BURGERS

EQUIPMENT

A meat grinder or KitchenAid stand
   mixer with grinding attachment

Two medium-size mixing bowls

A seasoned cast-iron skillet

A stiff spatula

A baking sheet

Parchment paper

A 4½-inch (12-cm) food ring or round
   cutter

Small metal bowls

THE BURGER

½ pound (225 g) slab bacon

1½ pounds (about 750 g) boneless chuck
   steak, marbled and close to 80/20

4 seeded white squishy buns, toasted
   (see instructions, page 33)

Beef tallow (rendered beef fat; see
   page 18)

Salt and black pepper, for seasoning

4 thick slices yellow cheddar cheese

THE TOPPINGS

Yellow mustard

Mayonnaise

1 medium Vidalia or Walla Walla onion,
   sliced

1 red beefsteak or heirloom tomato, sliced

Iceberg lettuce, shredded

1 Place the meat grinder or meat-grinding attachment in the freezer to chill for at least 30 minutes before using (or in your fridge overnight). This will help prevent the fat content in the bacon from melting and gumming up the grinder.

2 Take the fresh beef and bacon you've acquired from your good friend, the butcher, and chop them into roughly ½-inch or 1-inch (12-mm or 2.5-cm) chunks.

3 With the grinder running on low speed, add 4 to 5 chunks of beef to the grinder, followed by the same amount of bacon, alternating between the two until all the meat is ground. Be sure to have a medium mixing bowl in position to catch the ground meat.

4 Once all the meat is ground, swap the bowl of ground meat out for a clean bowl and put the meat through the grinder once more at the same speed. This will ensure that the bacon and beef are thoroughly combined. But never grind more than twice.

5 Transfer the bowl of twice-ground meat to the fridge to chill.

6 Meanwhile, prep each of the toasted bottom buns with a swipe of mustard, followed by a smear of mayonnaise, a few sliced onions, a slice of tomato, and a handful of shredded lettuce.

7 Preheat the cast-iron skillet over medium-high heat (or the flat top to medium-high) and add some beef tallow. Use the spatula to spread the fat, coating the surface.

8 Line a large baking sheet with parchment paper. Take the meat out of the fridge and divide it into 4 equal portions weighing approximately 8 ounces (250 g) each. On the lined sheet pan, lightly press each portion into the food ring, making sure each patty is equal in size and thickness. Be sure not to over press the meat—you'll want to maintain a somewhat loose grind to your patties.

9 When the skillet is hot, season the patties liberally with salt and pepper, place them in the pan, and let them cook for 5 minutes without disturbing them.

10 Flip the patties and cook for another 5 minutes. With about 1 minute to go, add a slice of cheese to each patty. Cover the skillet to accelerate the melt factor. When the patties are cooked through and the cheese is melty, transfer the patties to the prepared buns, add the top buns, and serve immediately.

TEXAS

THE SAN ANTONIO BEANBURGER

No, this is not the veggie burger you're thinking of. This is a beef burger, and a historically significant one at that. The beanburger is a true classic; indigenous to San Antonio, Texas, where it was born. In the 1950s the long-gone Sill's Snack Shack served the first Beanburger, and soon many local burger joints were copying them.

Good luck trying to find a beanburger outside of San Antonio. It never seemed to get past the city limits, and old-timers in the city of the Alamo are proud of their beanburger heritage. The original version from Sill's was a nod to Tex-Mex cooking, with a dollop of refried beans on top. Add to that a pile of Fritos and a swipe of Cheez Whiz and you can just imagine the flavors and textures going on.

One of the greatest interpretations of the beanburger in San Antonio is unquestionably the Macho Tostada at Chris Madrid's. A sight to behold, Madrid's version replaces the Fritos and Cheez Whiz with house-made corn chips and cascading melted cheddar. The late, great, Chris Madrid once explained to me that the beanburger was like "a burger and enchilada plate in one!" And it is. The hot refried beans soften the salty corn chips and work really well with the beefiness of the burger. The cheese acts as a sort of adhesive, keeping everything together.

My version of the beanburger walks the line between Madrid's and the classic at Sill's. Homemade refried beans is the right call, but how do you

Sill's Snack Shack, San Antonio, Texas

replace Fritos? Ideally, you don't because the Frito has no equal. In a pinch, substitute other salty store-bought corn chips, or better, pick up fresh tortilla chips from your local Mexican restaurant. For cheese my recipe again falls in the middle. Cheddar is great, but to get closer to the original make your own cheddar spread. If that's not your thing, simply drape your beanburger with a slice of cheddar and toss it under the broiler to melt before adding the top bun.

THE SAN ANTONIO BEANBURGER

MAKES 8 BURGERS

EQUIPMENT

A seasoned cast-iron skillet or a flat top

A stiff spatula

A medium-size mixing bowl

A #12 salad scoop

THE BURGER

Beef tallow (rendered beef fat; see page 18)

2 pounds (about 1 kg) fresh-ground 80/20 chuck

Salt, for seasoning

8 soft white buns, toasted (see instructions, page 33)

THE TOPPINGS

Frijoles Refritos de Jorge (refried beans, recipe follows)

Motz's Whiz Cheese Spread (recipe follows)

1 large bag (9¾ ounces/275 g) Fritos

1 medium Vidalia or Walla Walla onion, chopped

1 Make the frijoles refritos and cheese spread and set both aside.

2 Preheat the cast-iron skillet over medium heat (or a flat top to medium) and add some beef tallow. Use the spatula to spread the fat, coating the cooking surface.

3 Place the ground chuck in the mixing bowl. Using the salad scoop, form balls of beef (they should be heaping scoops), placing them on the heated skillet as you go. Each ball should have about 3 inches (7 cm) of space around it. (Depending on the size of your cooking surface, you may only be able to cook 2 or 3 burgers at a time.)

4 Sprinkle a generous pinch of salt on each ball of beef and then, using the stiff spatula, press them down *hard* until they're wide patties, just a bit larger than the bun. Once they're flat, don't touch them again. Let cook for 2½ minutes or until reddish liquid begins to form on the surface of the patty.

5 Flip the patties *once* and let them cook for another 2 minutes, undisturbed.

6 Spread a dollop of cheese spread on the toasted side of each bun (tops and bottoms) and add a handful of Fritos to each bottom bun.

7 When the burgers are cooked through, add them to the bottom buns followed by a healthy scoop of refried beans. Sprinkle with the chopped onion and top with the other half of the bun. Raise to lips, eat, and be transported to Southwest Texas.

FRIJOLES REFRITOS DE JORGE
Makes enough for 8 beanburgers

Refried beans are very easy to make, and if you like freshly made refried beans then you owe it to yourself to give this recipe a try. Unfortunately for the non-carnivores out there, the only way to elevate refried beans is by selling your soul to the pig—you'll need to use lard or bacon grease. Lard basically does two things to refried beans: It makes starchy, pasty beans luscious, and, of course, it adds tremendous flavor. Without bacon grease you're just trying to achieve that consistency and flavor by using oil and salt. Use lard for truly delicious refried beans.

1 (15-ounce/425-g) can pinto beans
¼ cup (60 ml) chicken broth, plus more if your beans become too thick
3 tablespoons (40 g) lard or bacon fat (if you don't want to buy lard, get a pack of bacon, cook the bacon, eat the bacon, and save the grease)
1 medium yellow onion, diced
1 tablespoon jalapeño (optional), seeded and diced
3 cloves garlic, minced
Sea salt, to taste

1 Drain the beans in a mesh sieve, transfer to a small mixing bowl, and mash with a potato masher until smooth. Add the chicken stock and continue to mash until a lumpy paste forms.
2 In a large saucepan, heat the lard over medium heat and add the diced onion. Cook until the onion is just translucent, about 5 minutes.
3 Add the jalapeño, if using, to the onions and cook for 2 minutes.
4 Add the garlic and cook for 1 minute.
5 Add the bean mixture, stir to incorporate, and cook for about 1 minute. Transfer to a food processor and pulse until fully blended and smooth. Return contents to the saucepan over low heat. Keep warm until ready to eat.

MOTZ'S WHIZ CHEESE SPREAD
Makes enough for 8 beanburgers

To construct a true San Antonio Beanburger you'll need to pick up some good-old processed Cheez Whiz. But for those who would prefer to avoid heavily processed foodstuffs, make your own Whiz with the recipe below, a variation on one of my favorite foods ever: cheese spread.

3 tablespoons (40 g) good, salted butter
3 tablespoons (25 g) all-purpose flour
1 cup (240 ml) half-and-half or light cream
1 teaspoon salt
8 ounces (225 g) extra-sharp cheddar, shredded

1 Start by making a roux: Melt the butter in a small saucepan over low heat. Stir in the flour and whisk constantly until the mixture becomes brown and smells nutty, about 3 minutes. (Do not overcook!)
2 Slowly stir in the half-and-half and salt, whisking continuously. When the cream has thickened slightly, add the shredded cheddar, one handful at a time, while continuously whisking. Yes, keep whisking.
3 Once the cheese is completely melted and the sauce is thick, remove it from the heat. Use it on your beanburgers immediately or store it in the fridge. It will last for a few days. It's also great on nachos, other burgers, or your finger.

MISSISSIPPI

THE SLUG BURGER

It's difficult to imagine that there was a time or place in modern American history when ground beef was not readily available. But hard times in the Deep South in the years leading up to the Great Depression took a toll on the all-beef patty that had grown in popularity only a decade earlier. It was not uncommon for burger joints to mix ground bread crumbs from day-old bread into their burger meat to extend the ground beef supply. The result was the oddly named "Slug Burger," so called, apparently, because you could pick one up for only a "slug," which was slang for a nickel at the time.

What happened next was magic.

As fate would have it, the breading mixed into the ground beef had a profound gastronomic effect—it acted as a sponge that soaked up grease from the griddle the burger was being fried upon. It would also crisp up the exterior of the patty faster, producing a scientific result that chefs know as the Maillard reaction. Of course, locals and regulars responded only to one thing—the great taste. So great that today, in many parts of rural Mississippi and in some remote pockets of the Deep South, the Slug Burger is alive and well.

The origins of the Slug Burger are murky, but its birthplace seems to be pinned to Corinth, Mississippi. Those who serve actual Slug Burgers today refuse to admit it or give up decades-old recipes. Almost a century ago, as the popularity of the Slug Burger flourished, short-order cooks would put their spin on the Slug using potato flour, soy grits, soy flour, and stale bread. Today there are meatpackers in northern Mississippi supplying many joints

Latham's Hamburger Inn, New Albany, Mississippi

with what has become an even more widely accepted Slug, a mixture of ground pork and soy flour (no beef and no bread crumbs).

You can still find great beef Slugs at places like Bill's Hamburgers, Latham's, and Phillips Grocery in northern Mississippi, though none of the owners will admit to adding anything to their ground beef and refuse to call them Slugs. And at Snappy Lunch in Mount Airy, North Carolina, ask for a hamburger and you'll get a pale patty that looks more bready than beefy. Snappy Lunch uses crumbled, cooked biscuits in their burgers. If you are looking for the non-Slug version at Snappy, you'll need to ask for the "hamburger with meat."

Now that I've piqued your interest, let's make some Slug Burgers. Since every Slug I've eaten contains super-secret ingredients, the recipe that follows is my approximation of what you might find on a road trip through northern Mississippi today.

THE SLUG BURGER

MAKES 6 BURGERS

EQUIPMENT

A seasoned cast-iron skillet or flat top

A medium-size mixing bowl

A stiff spatula

THE BURGER

Beef tallow (rendered beef fat; see
     page 18

1 pound (about 500 g) fresh-ground
     80/20 chuck

1 cup bread crumbs made by
     hand-crumbling day-old bread
     or fresh bread toasted until just
     dried out

Salt, for seasoning

6 soft white buns

THE TOPPINGS

Yellow mustard

Dill pickle chips

1 Preheat the cast-iron skillet over medium heat (or the flat top to medium) and add beef tallow.

2 Place the ground beef and bread crumbs in the mixing bowl and, using your hands, mix until fully blended. Divide the meat mixture into 6 equal portions (about 3 ounces/90 g each) and roll them into balls.

3 Place the balls of beef on the heated skillet. Each ball should have about 3 inches (7 cm) of space around it. (Depending on the size of your cooking surface, you may only be able to cook 2 or 3 at a time.)

4 Use the stiff spatula to give each of the balls a good press until it takes the shape of a patty (not quite as thin as the Griddle-Smashed Classic Cheeseburger on page 32, but close) and sprinkle each with a pinch of salt. Let cook, without disturbing them, for 3 minutes or until reddish liquid begins to form on the patty surface.

5 While the patties are cooking, prep the buns by slathering the cut-side of each bottom bun with a swipe of mustard and topping with 2 or 3 pickle chips—the traditional condiments for a classic slug burger.

6 Flip the burgers *once* and let them cook for another 1½ minutes without touching them. They will appear sizzling and crispy on their cooked sides when they're done. Transfer to the prepared buns and serve.

FLORIDA

THE CUBAN FRITA

The principle industry in Miami is tourism. Most people find their way to the warm weather during the winter months and don't give much thought to life in Miami beyond the beaches. For those smart enough to get off the sand and into the diverse and vibrant culture of Miami, one reward comes in the form of the Cuban frita.

In 1959, Cubans began to flee their country following the Cuban Revolution, and many settled in Miami, only about two hundred miles away. The frita was one of the culinary survivors of the exodus. Sharing the same DNA as the American hamburger, the frita was served from street carts in Havana before Fidel Castro seized control of the country. Chorizo spices such as paprika and garlic were mixed into the patty, and it was served on a soft roll with sautéed onions and a nest of fried potatoes on top.

Today many fritas can be found along Calle Ocho, the Miami street that runs directly through the proudly Cuban neighborhood of Little Havana. Some of the best can be found at El Rey de las Fritas. Every frita joint has its own take on the tasty Cuban burger, but all share a few key ingredients, like the fried potatoes and the chorizo-spiced beef. The classic Cuban bread roll is also key, similar in taste and texture to the pillowy-soft, thin-crunch exterior of po'-boy bread in New Orleans. Most importantly, the patty itself is cooked in a special sauce directly on the flat top—the secret ingredient that gives this burger a pronounced, caramelized kick.

Now here's the sad and crazy part: As far as we know, the frita no longer exists in Cuba. Mercedes Gonzalez, owner of El Rey, told me once, "There's

Drawing of a typical Frita stand, Havana, Cuba, pre-revolution 1950s, by Silvio

no way for them to find all of those ingredients!" It's almost as if a few smart Cubans stored the frita in a safe place (Miami) until the cloud of oppression blew over. Mercedes plans one day to open the first frita drive-thru in Cuba and reintroduce this salvaged tradition to the local population.

THE CUBAN FRITA

MAKES 8 BURGERS

EQUIPMENT

A medium-size mixing bowl

A saucepan or aluminum skillet with a heavy lid

A seasoned cast-iron skillet

A stiff spatula

THE TOPPINGS

Motz's Kinda-Secret Frita Sauce (recipe follows)

Thin-Cut Fried Potatoes (recipe follows)

Ketchup

THE BURGER

2 pounds (about 1 kg) fresh-ground 80/20 chuck

3 cloves garlic, minced

1 tablespoon paprika

¾ teaspoon ground cumin

¾ cup (95 g) grated onion (reserve ¼ cup/35 g for topping)

1 loaf Cuban bread or 8 Cuban rolls (any sturdy yet soft bakery rolls will work if you can't find Cuban bread)

Beef tallow (rendered beef fat; see page 18)

Salt, for seasoning

1 Prepare the frita sauce and fried potatoes according to the recipes opposite. I recommend starting with the sauce because it can simmer while the potatoes are frying. Set both aside.

2 In a mixing bowl, mix the ground beef, garlic, paprika, cumin, and grated onion, using your hands to blend until well combined.

3 Hand-form the mixture into 8 fairly thin (¼-inch/6-mm), loose, flat balls and set aside.

4 Slice the bread or rolls in half, then reassemble and place them, three at a time, in a dry saucepan with a heavy lid. Heat over low heat, covered, for approximately 10 minutes, flipping the bread once halfway through. If you're using rolls, they should be soft and steamy in the middle, but stiff and toasted on the outside.

5 Meanwhile, preheat the cast-iron skillet over medium or medium-low heat with some beef tallow, spreading it evenly over the surface with the spatula. Once the skillet is hot, add the patties, leaving 2 inches (5 cm) around them (you may only be able to fit two or three at a time), and press them flat like the Griddle-Smashed Classic Cheeseburger (page 32). Add a pinch of salt to each patty and let them cook for about 3 minutes, then flip.

6 Spoon a generous amount of the frita sauce over the burgers while they're sizzling in the skillet and let them cook for 2 minutes. Flip again and cook for 1 minute more.

7 Transfer the patties to the toasted bread or rolls. Top each patty with a heaping handful of fried potatoes, followed by a pinch of the reserved grated onion and a dollop of ketchup. Sandwich with the top piece of bread or roll and serve immediately.

MOTZ'S KINDA-SECRET FRITA SAUCE

Makes more than enough for 8 Cuban fritas

2 tablespoons olive oil
2 cloves garlic, crushed with a garlic press
2 ounces (55 g) tomato paste
½ teaspoon paprika
1 tablespoon sugar
2 tablespoons apple cider vinegar
2 tablespoons Frank's RedHot cayenne pepper sauce or similar hot sauce

1 Heat the olive oil in a saucepan over medium heat. Once the pan is hot, add the garlic and cook for about 1 minute, until it just begins to turn golden brown (do not burn).

2 Stir in the tomato paste and 1 cup (240 ml) water. Increase the heat to high and bring the liquid to a boil. Reduce the heat to a simmer and add the paprika, sugar, vinegar, and hot sauce. Stir to combine, cover, and simmer for 15 to 20 minutes. Remove from heat and set aside to cool.

3 Once cool to the touch, transfer the sauce to a blender and blend on low speed until smooth.

THIN-CUT FRIED POTATOES

Makes enough to top 8 Cuban fritas

EQUIPMENT

A deep frying pan
A mandoline slicer (optional)
A large mixing bowl or stockpot
Long tongs (skip the plastic tips!) or a metal slotted spoon

INGREDIENTS

1 quart (1 L) peanut or grapeseed oil (or enough to fill the frying pan with ½ inch/12 mm oil)
3 large russet (baking) potatoes
Ice water
Salt, for seasoning

1 Preheat the oil in the frying pan over medium-high heat until the top of the oil appears to be shimmering. It's hot enough if you add a piece of potato to the oil and it bubbles.

2 While the oil is heating, peel the potatoes and chop them into matchstick-size strips (or julienne them with a mandoline).

3 Place the matchstick potatoes in a large bowl or stockpot filled with enough ice water to cover them. Soak them for 15 minutes, then drain in a colander and pat dry with paper towels. WARNING: Make sure the potatoes are fairly dry before placing them in the oil (water + hot oil = horrible explosions).

4 Just a handful at a time, add the dry julienned potatoes to the hot oil in your frying pan. The oil should bubble up immediately upon contact.

5 Cook each batch for about 3 minutes or until golden brown, stirring occasionally. Using the tongs or a slotted spoon, remove the potatoes from the oil and place on a plate lined with paper towels.

6 Continue to fry handfuls of potatoes until they're all cooked, then transfer them to the mixing bowl (make sure it's dry first) and toss with salt to taste.

TENNESSEE

THE DEEP-FRIED BURGER

My obsession with exploring the myriad ways burgers are cooked and served in America started with the deep-fried burger. I mentioned to my good friend Brent Turner many years ago that I was thinking about making a documentary about hamburgers, and he told me, "You have to include Dyer's in Memphis." (His hometown.) "They actually deep-fry their burgers!" At first, I assumed it was just a gimmick dreamed up by a chef in search of something new. But what I discovered was a tiny gem of American culinary history.

In my travels throughout the United States I have since discovered other deep-fried burger joints, stands, and carts, and they all share one very important component—rich hamburger history. The method for deep-frying burgers was actually born of laziness: an accident-turned-tradition. One day, in around 1912, Elmer Dyer was too busy to drain the skillet he was using to cook burgers. Eventually the rendered fat became a deep pool of grease. Elmer discovered that if he strained the grease and used it to cook with, the result was actually a better-tasting burger.

Now I know what you are thinking—"Yikes! I'm not eating a deep-fried burger!" But trust me, you should, and you will. The deep-fried burger cooks in just 1 minute and, if the temperature of the oil is just right, the patty deflects most of the oil. These factors allow the patty to retain a moist composition and lend it a slightly crispy exterior.

To pull off this recipe you have two options—get your hands on some beef tallow (rendered beef fat) or simply use peanut oil in its place. Most

Dyer's original location, Memphis, Tennessee

burger joints that deep-fry burgers use tallow. Try it if you like, but be forewarned; cooking with large amounts of pure tallow creates an aroma that is not for everyone. It's also difficult to purchase in bulk. Some butchers will sell you suet, which is not rendered (they use it to add fat content to a lean grind of beef). Simply heat the suet and strain it, and you have tallow. Some claim cooking in beef tallow is better for you than any of the store-bought, highly refined hydrogenated oils out there. It's the way our ancestors ate.

When tallow is not readily available I use peanut oil, one of the best oils for deep-frying. However, be careful with this science experiment. Remember that deep-frying beef can be dangerous, since the liquid present in the raw patty will splatter and make for some impressive fireworks. Please follow the directions carefully.

THE DEEP-FRIED BURGER

**MAKES 8 QUARTER-POUND BURGERS
OR 4 DOUBLE-CHEESEBURGERS**

EQUIPMENT

A deep seasoned cast-iron skillet (don't
use a flat top)

A clean, smooth surface (a marble
countertop, or a 12 x 12-inch/30 x
30-cm marble floor tile, works well)

A stiff spatula

A wooden mallet or old-school wooden
potato masher

A mesh strainer for cleaning the oil

THE BURGER

1 quart (about 1 L) beef tallow or
enough peanut or grapeseed oil to fill
a skillet with 2 inches (5 cm) of oil

2 pounds (about 1 kg) fresh-ground
80/20 chuck

8 soft white hamburger buns

THE TOPPINGS

Yellow mustard to taste

2 to 3 medium sweet Vidalia or Walla
Walla onions, sliced paper-thin

Dill pickle chips

8 slices American cheese

1 Heat the tallow or oil in your skillet over medium heat.

2 While the oil is heating up, shape the ground beef into 8 portions on your clean, smooth work surface and roll them into equal-size balls (they should be slightly larger than golf balls). Chill on a plate in the refrigerator.

3 Prep the hamburger buns with a thin layer of mustard, a slice of onion, and a few pickle chips, and have them nearby. You'll want them open and ready for your deep-fried patties. The cheese, as well, should be within arm's reach of where you are frying.

4 Test the oil to see if it's ready: You'll know it's hot enough when a tiny pinch of beef bubbles immediately upon impact. Never put beef patties into a skillet of luke-warm grease or oil because the beef will just absorb it.

5 When the oil is ready, remove one of the balls of ground beef from the fridge and place it on your work surface. Dip the spatula into the oil to coat it, then squash the ball flat on the work surface (the oil will keep the meat from sticking to the spatula). Use the wooden smasher to press down on the back of the spatula to make that patty even thinner. A steady pressing and smoothing-out motion, starting in the middle of the meat and then sweeping out to the edges, works best. (If you pound the spatula down and try to lift it straight off the meat, the patty will likely break.) Try to keep your smashed patty round, but it

doesn't have to be perfect. (It takes practice to get this right). When you have a super-thin sheet of beef, approximately ⅛ inch (3 mm) thick, you are ready to fry.

6 Using the long edge of the spatula, carefully scrape the patty off of the work surface, starting with the edges. Try not to tear the meat.

7 Carefully transfer the flattened patty to the hot grease and watch the magic unfold. Within seconds the beef is reduced to a bun-size patty, and it is fully cooked after 1 minute in the oil. You can gently flip the patty in the oil after about 30 seconds; just be careful not to splash the oil. The first time I tried this, the oil was way too hot and the results were explosive. BE CAREFUL. If the oil seems too hot, lower the heat to just below medium.

8 When the patty is fully cooked, use the spatula to gently lift the it out of the grease, place a slice of American cheese on top, and briefly dip the patty back into the oil to melt the cheese. (This, too, takes practice. If your oil is too shallow, the cheese is likely to float off of the patty. If you can dip in a way that allows a quick wave of oil to wash over the cheese, you'll achieve the perfect melt factor.)

9 Place the fried cheeseburger patty on a prepped soft white bun and serve immediately. Repeat steps 5 through 8 with the remaining balls of ground beef and slices of cheese. You tell me if you think that was worth the effort. (It was.)

SOUTH CAROLINA

THE PIMENTO CHEESEBURGER

Unless you are from, or somehow connected to, the American South, you probably have zero appreciation for pimento cheese, and that is sad. I have many Southern relatives who are somewhat baffled that the great taste of pimento cheese has never made its way into common culinary vernacular north of the Mason-Dixon line, or beyond, for that matter. And I feel for them, because pimento cheese is awesome.

Southerners make sandwiches of a smear of pimento cheese on snow-white bread. They use it as a dip, or put it on crackers. You'd be hard pressed to find yourself at a party in the South where pimento cheese was not within snacking distance. But naturally, my favorite application for pimento cheese is on a burger.

When pimento cheese meets heat, all hell breaks loose. The properties of hot cheese and mayo do very well when applied to beef. Many Southern burger joints enthusiastically offer their take on this burger, and some of the best can be found in South Carolina, at places like the Fillin' Station in Hollywood, the Northgate Soda Shop in Greenville, and Rockaway Athletic Club in Columbia. Head to these places for the real deal; however, I've learned that a pimento cheeseburger is also a very gratifying thing to make at home.

There's not much to pimento cheese, but the glorious combination of mayonnaise, diced pimentos, and sharp cheddar is pure dairy alchemy. It's one of my favorite burgers to make and has a slight twist.

If you are fortunate enough to live in the South, then you have access to the great store-bought Palmetto Cheese from Pawleys Island, South Carolina (a play on words—the palmetto is a species of palm tree native to the southern United States). It really is about as good as it gets, but if you need to make your own "Pimena Cheese" (as it's correctly pronounced down South), I've included my mother's recipe on page 195.

THE PIMENTO
CHEESEBURGER

MAKES 4 CHEESEBURGERS

EQUIPMENT

A seasoned cast-iron skillet

A stiff spatula

A medium-size mixing bowl

A #12 salad scoop

THE BURGER

Beef tallow (rendered beef fat; see
    page 18)

1 pound (about 500 g) fresh-ground
    80/20 chuck

Salt, for seasoning

4 soft white buns, toasted (see instruc-
    tions, page 33)

THE TOPPINGS

1 beefsteak tomato, sliced

Iceberg lettuce, shredded

Mama's Pimena Cheese (recipe follows)

1 Preheat the cast-iron skillet over medium heat and add some beef tallow. Use the spatula to spread the fat, coating the surface of the pan.

2 Place the ground beef in a mixing bowl and, using the salad scoop, make heaping balls of beef, placing them on the heated skillet as you go. Each ball should have about 3 inches (7 cm) of space around it. (Depending on the size of your cooking surface, you may only be able to cook 2 or 3 burgers at a time.)

3 Add a generous pinch of salt to each ball of beef and, using the stiff spatula, press them down *hard* until they're wide patties just a bit larger than the buns. Let them cook, without disturbing them, for 2½ minutes or until reddish liquid begins to form on the surface of the patty.

4 Prep the toasted buns with a slice of tomato on each bottom bun followed by a handful of shredded lettuce. Set aside.

5 Flip the burgers *once* and don't press them again. Add a healthy dollop of Mama's pimena cheese to each patty and let them cook for another 2 minutes.

6 Transfer the cheesy patties to the prepared buns and serve immediately.

MAMA'S PIMENA CHEESE
Makes enough to make you happy

- 1 (8-ounce/225-g) block of sharp cheddar cheese, shredded (don't use preshredded cheese)
- 4 ounces (115 g) cream cheese, softened
- ½ cup (120 ml) mayonnaise
- 1 (4-ounce/115-g) jar pimentos, finely chopped
- 2 tablespoons sriracha chili sauce

In a large mixing bowl, mix the cheddar, cream cheese, mayonnaise, chopped pimentos, and sriracha with a spatula until everything is combined and chunky—not smooth. Best used fresh.

NORTH CAROLINA

THE CAROLINA SLAW BURGER

When I think of the great road food of North Carolina, pulled pork sandwiches immediately come to mind. Served on soft untoasted buns, the pulled pork sandwich of the celebrated out-of-the-way pig joints usually comes standard with a big dollop of creamy coleslaw. That coleslaw is not served as a side, however; it's presented on the sandwich. In my mind, this equals borderline healthy eating—at least I'm getting some veggies. It probably didn't take long for someone to apply the same treatment to a burger, specifically a chili cheeseburger, giving birth to a Southern legend.

Depending on where you're eating, there are two basic ways the Carolina slaw burger is prepared. Some are made with a red slaw, in which the mayonnaise component is swapped out for ketchup. But for the most part, a mayo-based slaw is the predominant choice. Then there's the chili, which is usually a thin, beanless beef stew. But wait, there's more. To be a fully realized slaw burger it must also have mustard, cheese, and chopped onion. You are probably thinking this sounds like a ridiculous mess (which it is), but the Carolina slaw burger goes down with ease.

One of my favorite places to get a true Carolina Slaw Burger is at Duke's Grill in Monroe, North Carolina. Duke's has been making the slaw burger since 1951, and not much has changed since Duke served his first one. His nephew Dennis started working at Duke's when he was nine years old,

Duke's Grill, Monroe, North Carolina

eventually bought the place, and changed very little. "I made the chili better, that's about it," he told me once, "by adding beef." Apparently the original "chili" sauce his uncle used was nothing more than ketchup, mustard, and hot sauce. Dennis's chili is far better.

To me tradition trumps all, so embrace the chaos you are about to create. But if a hot, creamy mess is not your thing, I would recommend toasting the buns to keep the burger from becoming a knife-and-fork affair past the second bite.

1751

THE CAROLINA SLAW BURGER

MAKES 8 BURGERS

EQUIPMENT

A seasoned cast-iron skillet or flat top

A stiff spatula

A medium-size mixing bowl

A #12 salad scoop

THE BURGER

Beef tallow (rendered beef fat; see
   page 18)

2 pounds (about 1 kg) fresh-ground
   80/20 chuck

Salt, for seasoning

8 slices American cheese (preferably
   deli-sliced, not prepackaged
   "singles")

8 soft white buns or potato buns,
   toasted (see instructions,
   page 33)

THE TOPPINGS

Stupid-Easy Cole Slaw (page 308)

Beanless Beef Chili Sauce (page 284)

½ cup (65 g) finely chopped sweet
   Vidalia or yellow onion

Yellow mustard

1 Make the coleslaw and chili sauce according to recipe instructions and set aside.

2 Preheat the cast-iron skillet over medium heat (or a flat top to medium) and add some beef tallow. Use the spatula to spread the fat, coating the cooking surface.

3 Put the ground beef in the mixing bowl and, using the salad scoop, make heaping balls of beef, placing them on the heated skillet as you go. Each ball should have about 3 inches (7 cm) of space around it.

3 Add a generous pinch of salt to each ball of beef and, using the stiff spatula, press them down *hard* until they're wide patties just a bit larger than the buns. Let them cook, without disturbing them, for 2½ minutes or until reddish liquid begins to form on the surface.

4 Flip the patties *once* and don't press them again. Add a slice of cheese to each patty and let them cook for another 2 minutes.

5 Add a swipe of mustard to the toasted side of each top bun. Set aside.

6 When the burgers are cooked through, it's time to put all the pieces together. (Pay attention: The success of your slaw burger is dependent upon its construction.) Start by placing a heaping scoop of coleslaw on the bottom half of each toasted bun. Top the slaw with a cheeseburger patty, a healthy scoop of chili sauce, the chopped onion, and the top half of the bun. Consume immediately.

Hot Beef
...ennial
...nd Co...

REGIONAL FAVORITES

THE
NORTHEAST

PENNSYLVANIA
THE FLUFF SCREAMER

It may sound like a joke or an attention-grabbing stunt burger dreamed up for social media fame, but this is an actual regional burger and as such needs to be properly appreciated. From the heart of working-class Pennsylvania coal country comes a burger that is more science project than culinary delight, a burger oozing with pride (and sticky marshmallow goo): the Fluff Screamer. Two words I thought I'd never see together, but I'm sure glad I have.

Visit Girardville, Pennsylvania, and you'll find yourself at the center of the Fluff Screamer universe. This strange concoction was invented in the 1970s when a sixteen-year-old girl would regularly visit and ask for Fluff on her burger. While Tony's stocked the classic marshmallow spread for their hot chocolate, the staff would refuse to honor her request. Legend has it that eventually Tony's niece, a waitress at the time, made it for her one day and people began to order the same. Half a century later the legend endures.

Originally, Tony's was well-known for a burger simply known as the Screamer. For reasons that may be obvious, the name certainly fits; Screamer sauce, invented in the 1940s, is screaming hot. At its core, it's a tomato-based chile sauce that's more paste than sauce. There are other versions of this sauce found throughout Schuylkill County; all are slightly different, and at least one, Pop's Original, is available by mail order if you want to try the real thing. The second ingredient on the Pop's label is "hot dogs"—likely a proletarian coal country substitute for beef and,

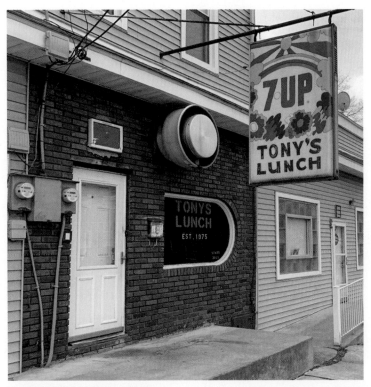

Tony's Lunch, Giardville, Pennsylvania

unquestionably, a very flavorful way to make a meat sauce. My sidebar recipe here is loosely based on what I've had and definitely includes hot dogs.

Now let's put the ingredients together and make a Fluff Screamer. To stay completely authentic there is only ONE way to make this burger, and attention to detail is paramount. If you are not using a griddled fresh beef patty, Screamer sauce, a slice of cold white American cheese, diced raw onion, a dollop of soft butter, and Marshmallow Fluff on an untoasted white burger bun, you are doing it wrong. The science of atomic chili sauce and sticky-sweet marshmallow spread is real, and, not surprisingly, the two both cancel out and enhance each other: the sweet marshmallow tames the heat while the chili softens the sugar overload. And naturally, the rendered beef fat and butter create balance. Get ready to both confuse and excite your taste buds and eat like a Central Pennsylvania coal miner.

THE FLUFF SCREAMER

MAKES 4 BURGERS

EQUIPMENT

4 (8-inch/20-cm) parchment paper
squares

A seasoned cast-iron skillet

THE BURGER

1 pound (about 500 g) fresh-ground
80/20 beef

Beef tallow (rendered beef fat; see page
18), enough to lubricate the pan

Kosher salt or good sea salt

Screamer Sauce (recipe follows)

4 classic white no-frills burger buns

8 slices white American cheese

1 medium sweet onion (white, Vidalia,
or Spanish), diced

Butter, at room temperature
(spreadable)

1 (7.5-ounce/213 g) jar classic Marshmallow Fluff

1 Divide the beef into 4 equal portions
(4 ounces/125 g) each.

2 Then, using 2 squares of parchment
paper, hand-smash each portion between
the sheets until they are about ⅛ inch
(3 mm) thick.

3 Heat a smear of beef tallow in the skillet
over medium-high heat and, when it starts
to smoke, add 2 of the patties.

4 Add a pinch of salt to each patty and let
cook for about 3 minutes.

5 Flip and cook for another minute, then
repeat with the other 2 patties.

6 Warm Screamer Sauce ever so slightly
and prepare your ingredients for assembly.
Here is the very important order of elements to create the perfect Fluff Screamer:
A On the untoasted heel of the bun, place a
cooked burger patty.
B If you are including what is referred
to in Girardville, Pennsylvania, as "quick
cheese" (unmelted), place 2 slices here.
C On top of that, add a dollop of Screamer
Sauce and a handful of the diced onion.
D On the inside of the crown of the bun,
smear the soft butter, followed immediately
by an even larger wad of Fluff.

7 Take a bite and you may (or may not)
become a believer.

SCREAMER SAUCE

Makes enough for about 20 Fluff Screamers

There is no printed recipe for this very locally famous sauce from Central Pennsylvania. However, it is agreed that this sauce is basically a meat-based, spicy, hot chile paste. The recipe below is my interpretation of that sauce. It includes hot dogs and requires a blender or food processor. This recipe is definitely not as insanely hot as screamer sauces from PA. If you require more heat, add extra cayenne and hot sauce at your own risk.

2 tablespoons vegetable oil
1 medium onion, diced
1 medium green bell pepper, diced
5 hot dogs, chopped into discs
1½ tablespoons chile powder
1 teaspoon garlic powder
2 teaspoons cayenne pepper flakes
1 (15-ounce/425-g) can tomato sauce
2 tablespoons tomato paste
½ cup (120 ml) water, plus some extra to thin
2 tablespoons hot pepper sauce (like Frank's RedHot or Texas Pete)

1 Heat a skillet over medium heat and add the vegetable oil.

2 When the oil is heated, sauté the onion and green pepper until softened, about 4 minutes.

3 Add the hot dogs and all the dry spices (chili powder, garlic powder, and cayenne) and stir to incorporate. Cook for an additional 5 minutes.

4 Add the tomato sauce, tomato paste, and water, reduce the heat, cover, and simmer for 10 minutes, stirring every few minutes.

5 If after 10 minutes the sauce is still liquidy, uncover and cook for a few minutes more.

6 Remove from the heat and allow to cool.

7 Add the hot pepper sauce and transfer to a blender or food processor. Pulse until a paste-like consistency forms. Drizzle more water if it's getting too thick, but be cautious: the finished sauce should spread like a paste and not be too runny.

NEW YORK

KORZO'S DEEP-FRIED LÁNGOS BURGER

My good friends Maria and Otto Zizak at Korzo of Brooklyn have already given us the only veggie burger I will eat (see the Beet Burger, page 320), but let's talk about the reason I know them in the first place (spoiler alert: it was not the veggie burger). This is one of the most unusual burgers I've ever eaten and is a fun science experiment to try at home. Time to impress your friends and family with the tasty deep-fried lángos burger.

I've come across plenty of dough-wrapped, deep-fried foods in my extensive global eating adventures. Many, many foodways of the world have some version of filled, cooked dough, most of it street food and all of it tasty. The list is enormous, but consider the Brazilian pastel, the Southern fruit-filled hand pie, the Cornish pasty, kolaches, dumplings, pierogis, potstickers, and empanadas just to name a few. There's even the crumbly loose beef-and-cabbage-stuffed bierock (see recipe, page 98), which goes back to the beginning of the nineteenth century, invented by Germans living along the Volga River in Russia. When we define the burger, it is understood that Americans were the first to make the Hamburg steak portable by serving it on bread. But the beef-filled bierock predates that invention by almost a hundred years, loosely challenging (no pun intended) the established history of the hamburger.

Slovak or Hungarian lángos bread is a fried flatbread that may go back as far as the days of the Turkish Empire. It is a popular street snack,

stretched round, fried in oil, and served either plain or topped with things like sour cream and shredded cheese, sort of like a pizza. The fried dough is similar in taste and texture to a donut.

At first, I was skeptical about the lángos burger at Korzo, but I knew the quality had to be there based on Chef Maria's deep resume. Maria cooks for the Slovakian delegation when the UN is in session. She's a true Slovak chef, and her bryndzové halušky (a traditional dish of potato dumpling and sheep cheese) has been called the best in the United States.

Otto and Maria wanted to create something that combined their love of the American burger with a familiar taste of home. It's a grilled burger wrapped in dough with condiments tucked inside. The entire thing is dunked in hot oil for a minute and fried until golden brown, allowing the cheese inside to become melty. And because the Zizaks are Slovakian, the condiments are distinctly European—good mustard, bacon, pickles, and Emmentaler cheese. In reality, you can put whatever you want in your lángos burger as long as it doesn't explode in the hot oil.

Also, this burger can be made in your kitchen, but to be safe (and to make it authentically char-grilled), let's take this one outside.

KORZO'S DEEP-FRIED LÁNGOS BURGER

MAKES 3 BURGERS

EQUIPMENT

A large mixing bowl or standing mixer with a dough hook or paddle attachment

A small saucepan

A wooden spoon or rubber spatula

A clean kitchen towel

A clean, smooth surface for kneading and rolling out the dough

A 4-inch (10-cm) food ring or round cutter

3 (8-inch/20-cm) parchment paper squares

A charcoal chimney

Charcoal

A charcoal grill

A grill brush

A small, well-seasoned cast-iron skillet

Paper towels

A plate and small sheet pan

A deep cast-iron pan or pot for deep-frying

A long-handled grill spatula/turner

A slotted (or mesh) metal spoon

THE DOUGH

2 cups (240 g) all-purpose flour, plus extra for dusting

½ teaspoon salt

½ teaspoon sugar

¼ cup (60 ml) whole milk, warm

2 teaspoons active dry yeast

½ cup (120 ml) sour cream

1 tablespoon canola or vegetable oil

THE BURGER

1 pound (about 500 g) fresh-ground 80/20 chuck

3 slices thick-cut bacon

1 to 2 quarts (1 to 2 L) fry oil (peanut, canola, or corn), enough to fill your pan halfway

Salt, for seasoning

3 slices Emmentaler cheese

Dill pickle chips

Some good European mustard

Note: I called Otto asking for Maria's dough recipe. Instead, he sent me a list of ingredients and, laughing, told me to "figure it out!" So, this is *not* Maria's recipe but is a lángos recipe of my invention based on Maria's ingredients.

1 Make the dough first, leaving enough time for it to rise (1 hour, or until doubled in size). In a large bowl or standing mixer add the flour, salt, and sugar. Stir until combined.

2 In a small saucepan, heat the milk over low heat until warm (120°F/50°C). Don't let it boil or become too hot because it will kill your yeast!

3 Add the yeast and sour cream to the flour mixture. Mix with a wooden spoon or spatula, or on low speed with the dough hook of your standing mixer, while slowly adding in the warm milk. Continue until the dough forms a ball but doesn't stick to the sides of the bowl. (If your dough is too sticky, add more flour. Too crumbly after adding all the milk? Add a little warm water.)

4 Still in the bowl, form the dough into a ball and drizzle the oil over the top, turning to coat the dough's surface.

5 Cover the bowl with a clean kitchen towel and set in a warm spot to rise (1 hour, or until doubled in size).

6 While you're waiting for the dough to rise, it's time to heat the grill and cook the meat. First, prepare your burger patties: Divide the ground beef into 3 equal portions (roughly 5.3 ounces/166 g each).

7 Place the food ring on a cutting board or clean surface lined with parchment paper and add a portion of beef. Gently press the beef into the ring to create a perfectly round patty. (I use the ring for consistent thickness, but you can eyeball the size if you prefer. Both methods work fine. Just be sure not to over-press the meat—you want it to maintain a somewhat loose grind.)

8 Repeat for the other 2 portions of beef and put the patties in the fridge until you're ready to grill.

9 Using the chimney starter, light the charcoal. When coals are ready, transfer them to the grill, making sure that the bottom vent is open. Spread the coals out, leaving a small space on one side (as a cooler rest spot in case things get too hot in there).

10 Place the grate over the coals and, using a grill brush, scrape off any residual buildup. Cover the grill and make sure that the top vent is wide open. Place your cast-iron skillet on the grill and then give both some time to heat up—first into the fire will be the bacon.

11 While everything is heating, grab a plate, line it with paper towels, and keep it nearby.

12 When the skillet is hot, add the bacon (slide to the cool side of the grill if it gets too hot).

13 Flip and cook until done, removing to your paper towel–lined landing pad nearby. Pro Tip: Use the Bacon in the Round recipe (page 294) instead of breaking your bacon strips into pieces—this is not a burger where you can afford to have bacon bits poking out the sides.

14 Remove the skillet from the grill and resume heating until your grill grate is ridiculously hot. While your grill is getting back up to speed, get your frying setup going.

15 Fill a deep, cast-iron pot with oil to about halfway up the wall or the container and heat to 375°F (190°C), but no higher (when oil gets above 400°F/205°C things get dangerous).

16 At this point, and not before, grab your burger patties from the fridge and season both sides with a liberal amount of salt and pepper.

17 Place the patties on the hot grill grate, cover the grill, and leave them alone. Allow the patties to cook for about 3 minutes. The cooking time can vary depending on environmental and equipment factors, so you'll have to use your best judgment here. A good visual cue is when you see red liquid start to form on the uncooked surface of the burger; then it's time to flip. Take a peek just shy of that 3-minute mark.

18 Flip the patties and cook (again, untouched and covered) for an additional 2 minutes.

19 Transfer the cooked patties to a plate and bring inside along with your cooked bacon. Set both aside.

20 Back to the lángos dough! Punch down the risen dough, getting out any large air bubbles.

21 On a clean, flour-dusted surface, knead the dough briefly and then divide into 3 equal portions.

22 Roll each portion into a ball and set aside to rest, covered, for about 10 minutes.

23 This is a good time to sit down for a second, take a sip of your hopefully still-cold beer, and wipe the sweat off your brow. You're almost there—don't give up! You're doing great.

24 Next, roll out each dough ball and stretch into a roughly 8-inch (20-cm) round, similar to the way you would make a pizza. The dough should be free of any holes or thin sections—this is critical to your success.

25 Assemble each burger upside down in the center of the dough: Start with the cheese, then add the bacon and pickles. Smear some mustard onto a patty and place it mustard-side down on top. Make sure there are no sharp pieces protruding, as they will definitely poke holes in your plan.

26 Pull the edges of the dough up and around the burger, bringing them together in the center of the patty. Twist and pinch the edges to form a seam. (Use a bit of warm water here if the dough is not sticky enough to close.)

27 By now your oil should be good and hot, but before you fry, prepare a clean baking sheet or plate lined with paper towels and keep nearby.

28 Using a slotted spoon, slowly lower the first dough-wrapped burger into the hot oil, making sure the oil is not in danger of overflowing. The burger should bob in the oil.

29 Cook for roughly 30 seconds and then flip gently, just like a donut. The complete cooking time is roughly 1 minute, so do not walk away.

30 When it's perfectly golden brown, transfer the burger to your sheet pan lined with paper towels and give it a minute to cool down. Repeat steps 28 through 30 with the remaining 2 burgers.

31 Slice open and eat immediately.

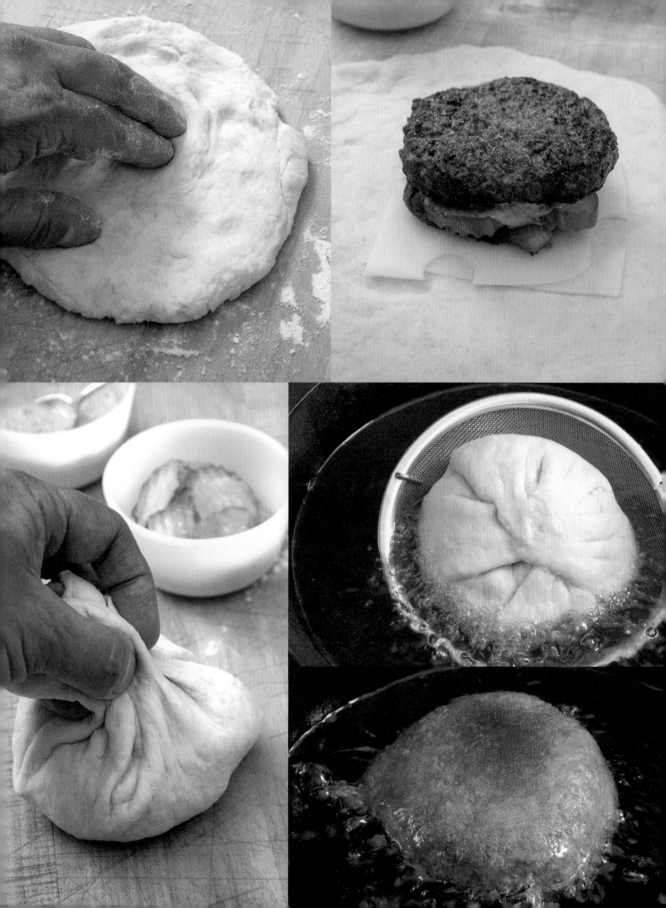

THE GARGIULO BURGER

There are a handful of places to get an old-school, hot roast beef sandwich in Brooklyn, New York, but some of the best come from the south end of Nostrand Avenue in the neighborhood of Sheepshead Bay. Brennan and Carr has been open since 1938 and has not changed much about the way they do things there. The waiters still wear ties and white jackets, the beer on tap is ice cold, and the roast beef is made every day in-house. Places like Roll-N-Roaster nearby and John's Deli both make excellent hot roast beef sandwiches, but Brennan and Carr, with almost ninety years in the roast beef business, is hard to beat. And it's all about the dipping station.

A visit to Brennan and Carr in Brooklyn is an absolute must. You enter basically through the open kitchen, and it's a full-frontal assault on the senses: the crew hard at work, the deep aroma of roasted beef, and the famous trough of beef broth in the center of it all. If you ask for yours "dipped," a pair of tongs sends the sandwich for a quick dunk in the beef broth. But for me it's the double-dip.

There is a burger on the menu at Brennan and Carr that was an accidental invention. Today it's one of their biggest sellers—the Gargiulo Burger. As the origin story goes, decades ago the one-hundred-year-old upscale Coney Island Italian restaurant and banquet hall needed a place to feed their very large crew after work on Sunday. The owners were friends with Brennan and Carr, who would put out large trays of roast beef and burger patties to keep things simple. The Gargiulo family would bring their own Italian loaves, and at some point someone put both roast beef and burger

Staff at Brennan and Carr, Brooklyn, New York, circa 1958

together. Today if you order the Gargiulo Burger it comes with their house-made sliced roast beef, sautéed Spanish onions, a griddled burger patty, and American cheese. The entire thing gets a dip in the broth bath and comes out one gloriously hot, wet mess. Prepare to be genuinely impressed by the beauty and simplicity of this burger. Be sure to have more napkins than you think you'll need nearby.

THE GARGIULO BURGER

MAKES 4 BURGERS

EQUIPMENT

A seasoned cast-iron skillet

A 4-inch (10-cm) food ring or round
 cutter

4 (8-inch/20-cm) parchment paper
 squares

A stiff spatula or turner

A medium-sized stockpot

Metal tongs

THE BURGER

1 pound (about 500 g) fresh-ground
 80/20 chuck

3 quarts really good beef broth

1 tablespoon butter

4 sturdy hard rolls (Kaiser or similar)

Salt, for seasoning

1 pound (about 500 g) high-quality deli-
 sliced roast beef

Caramelized Onions (see recipe,
 page 54)

8 slices American cheese

1 Divide the beef into 4 equal parts (4 ounces/125 g each).

2 Place the food ring on a cutting board or hard surface lined with a parchment square and add a portion of beef. Gently press the beef into the ring to create a perfectly round patty. (I use the ring for consistent thickness, but you can eyeball the size if you prefer. Just be sure not to over-press the meat—you want to maintain a somewhat loose grind.)

3 Remove the ring and set aside. Repeat steps 2 and 3 to form the other 3 patties.

4 Add the beef broth to the stockpot and set over low heat, to warm. Don't let it boil, and cover until ready to use.

5 Heat the cast-iron skillet over medium heat and add a pat of butter.

6 Once melted and bubbling, add the buns to the pan, cut-sides down, to toast.

7 Check on them every minute or so; remove them from the pan once they're perfectly golden brown. Set aside.

8 Raise the heat under your skillet to medium-high. Once hot, salt the patties on both sides and place them in pan; they should sizzle loudly when they hit the pan. Cook for 3 minutes, undisturbed. The goal here is to sear the burgers, sealing in the juices. When you see red liquid start to form on the uncooked surface of the burgers, it's time to flip.

9 Reduce the heat to medium and cook for an additional minute (again, do not disturb them while cooking).

10 Find some space in the pan to heat up the roast beef. Divide into 4 equal parts, heat for barely a minute, flip, and heat for another minute. Then place the roast beef atop the flipped patties.

11 Place a wad of the caramelized onions on top of the roast beef (use my recipe on page 54, but to be as authentic as Brennan and Carr, use Spanish onion and slice them thicker).

12 Then add 2 slices of American cheese on top of that. Cover to melt the cheese.

13 Transfer each pile of beef, onions, and cheese to the bottom bun of a toasted roll and add the top bun.

14 Using the tongs, get a good grip on the whole burger and dunk the entire thing into the broth, quickly (do not linger in the broth). Make sure the broth is not boiling or it will overflow (trust me here). And of course, to make my favorite Gargiulo Burger, dip it a second time.

NEW YORK

THE CHESTER-ROUER

Growing up at the beach on Long Island gave me the opportunity to be an ocean lifeguard when I became fifteen years old. To this day, I still say that it was the dreamiest job I've ever had. To sit high on a lifeguard bench, in the summer sun, watching the waves, was exactly how I wanted to spend my days, and I still think about it often. I also think about the Chester.

On breaks from "saving lives" at the surf club in Quogue, we would get exercise by running down the beach. It just so happened that a neighboring private beach club had a burger called the Chester Special on their lunch menu, which I craved. We would run down the beach, scarf two of them as fast as possible, and run back to work.

The Chester Special was invented one booze-fueled night by a bunch of teens looking for late-night sustenance. They had ground beef and cheese, but no buns. A guy named Roger Moley improvised with some toasted, buttered bread, and a legend was born. The next day, his buddy Chester Murray brought the idea to the beach club and asked if the kitchen could make him another for lunch. From that point on, when anyone wanted this simple three-ingredient concoction, they called for a Chester. That was more than fifty years ago, and the tiny, private beach club has probably served over a quarter million Chesters since then.

Is the Chester a patty melt? Not really. A traditional patty melt has very specific ingredients (see the Classic Patty Melt, page 110). It's unquestionably in the patty melt *family* but closer to a classic grilled cheese with a burger patty shoved inside. It's perfect. The diner chain Friendly's has a

Joe Rouer in the kitchen, Joe Rouer's Bar, Luxembourg, Wisconsin

very similar burger on their menu called the Set-Up, but their version adds some grilled onions. This got me thinking one day, as I was experimenting after a visit to the Upper Wisconsin burger outpost Joe Rouer's Bar. Their signature burger has a secret cooking method that I may have unlocked. I believe the burger patties at Rouer are cooked in a pan with chopped onions and beef broth. The result is pure alchemy, as the beef fat renders and mixes with the broth and onions. I too was short on buns that day and reached for some classic white bread and American cheese, and the Chester-Rouer was realized. It is one of the greatest burgers I've ever made.

THE CHESTER-ROUER

MAKES 3 CHEESEBURGERS

EQUIPMENT

2 (8-inch/20-cm) parchment paper
squares

2 large seasoned cast-iron skillets

2 spatulas/turners

THE BURGER

12 ounces (340 g) fresh-ground 80/20
chuck

1 cup (240 ml) beef broth, plus more on
standby

1 medium sweet onion (white, Vidalia,
or Spanish), chopped

Butter, softened

6 slices sturdy sandwich white bread
or Pullman bread

6 slices American cheese

1 Scoop the beef into 3 balls. Then, using 2 squares of parchment paper, hand-smash the balls between the sheets until they are thin and wide.

2 Add 1 cup of the broth to the first cast-iron skillet and bring to a simmer over medium heat.

3 Add the chopped onion to the simmering broth and cook for 4 minutes.

4 Next, add the thin-smashed patties to the broth and onions and cook for about 3 minutes. You can crowd as many patties as possible in the pan because they are going to shrink pretty quickly.

5 Flip the patties and cook for another few minutes. If the broth is evaporating, add some more to the pan. If it's getting a little thick, that's good: that's where the flavor is hiding.

6 Butter one side of each slice of bread and set aside. You're creating pairs here: 2 slices of bread equals 1 Chester-Rouer.

7 Heat the second skillet over medium-low heat and add as many pairs of bread slices as will fit, all butter-sides down. (You will likely have to do this in batches.)

8 Place a slice of cheese on top of each slice of bread.

9 Next, top half of your cheesy bread slices with a cooked patty from the first skillet and some of those tasty cooked onion bits!

10 Once you have your patties set up, flip the bread slices with cheese *only* on top of the patties. Hopefully, at this point, the cheese has melted a bit.

11 Let cook for a minute or so. Then use 2 spatulas to carefully flip the burger over in the skillet. The bread should be golden brown and cooked perfectly. If not, keep flipping until both sides look perfect.

THE CHESTER SPECIAL

To make a classic Chester, skip the broth steps. Using both pans, create open-faced grilled cheeses in one and cook the patties with a sprinkle of salt in the other. Simply marry the two and eat. Prepare to be dumbfounded by its perfection.

Chester Murray and his Chester Special

CONNECTICUT

THE STEAMED CHEESEBURG

In all of my research and rambling around America, I have yet to find a burger-cooking method as unusual as the steamed cheeseburger. Sometimes affectionately referred to as a "cheeseburg" in its birthplace of central Connecticut, this burger is exactly what it sounds like—a patty of ground beef that has been steamed throughout and draped with molten hot steamed cheese. I know what you're thinking—no griddle char? Not here. The preparation of some of the best steamed cheeseburgs in Connecticut involves a custom-made midcentury stainless-steel steaming contraption; a boxy stovetop chamber that generates a substantial amount of steam and renders each patty a color that some have said resembles a wet gray woolen sock. An unfortunate but accurate description. But this method creates a super-moist burger that has a pronounced beefy profile like no other. And when this moist patty is paired with hot cheddar cheese, you may just forgive the lack of sear from an open flame.

At one point in its long history, Connecticut was the center of industrial America. Factories produced much of the silverware, firearms, and clocks that Americans used, and the machines that made these things were invented and perfected in Connecticut as well. These included the milling machines, lathes, forge drop hammers, and gear shapers that became the backbone of the state's identity and the foundation of America's nineteenth-century manufacturing growth and expansion. It makes perfect sense that the metal box created to steam burgers was conceived here, too.

Jack's Lunch, Middletown, Connecticut

In the 1930s, a young man set up a homemade steaming box outside a diner named Jack's Lunch in Middletown. Its proximity to the factories of central Connecticut made the steamed cheeseburg a favorite of shift workers. Eventually, the cheeseburg production moved into Jack's Lunch and the rest was history.

Today, one of the greatest examples of this truly unique cheeseburger tradition can be found at Ted's Restaurant in Meriden, Connecticut. They no longer feed shift workers at three A.M. (just about every aspect of factory life has vanished in this part of America due to business moving overseas), but generations of steamed cheeseburg devotees still line up outside at lunchtime.

You've probably guessed already: I am the proud owner of an official steam box for cheeseburgs, courtesy of Ted's Restaurant. Although this is the best and most authentic way to produce a steamed cheeseburg, you do not have to own one to make them at home.

THE STEAMED CHEESEBURG

MAKES 6 BURGERS

EQUIPMENT

A large multistage steaming stockpot with two steaming colander inserts and a cover

2 small heatproof ramekins for melting the cheese

Long tongs (skip the plastic tips!)

THE BURGER

2 pounds (about 1 kg) fresh-ground 80/20 chuck (ask your butcher for a loose grind)

Salt, for seasoning

½ pound (225 g) mild white cheddar cheese, cut into 1-ounce (30-g) cubes

6 small Kaiser rolls (you'll want something substantial here—that hot cheese needs support)

THE TOPPINGS

Green-leaf lettuce

1 or 2 medium sweet Vidalia or Walla Walla onions, sliced

Yellow mustard

Ketchup and mayo (to be fully authentic)

1 Place ¾ inch (2 cm) of water in the bottom of the stockpot and bring to a gentle boil.

2 Divide the ground beef into 6 equal portions and hand-form each into roughly ½-inch (12-mm) thick patties.

3 When the water is boiling, it's time to cook the burgers. I recommend cooking two at a time. After each batch add a bit more water to the pot. An audible clue to little or no water in the pot is that you'll hear rendered fats sizzling. Nothing should be sizzling in there.

4 Salt both sides of the patties just before placing them into the first steamer insert. Lower the insert into the stockpot, cover, and let cook for 8 minutes. Resist the temptation to remove the lid during steaming. Keeping the steam robust is key.

5 While the burger patties are steaming, add a 1-ounce (30-g) cube of cheese to each ramekin.

6 When 8 minutes are up, lift the lid (it's okay, you have my permission now), and add the second steaming insert to your stockpot, placing the two cheese-filled ramekins inside. Cover and let cook for 6 minutes more.

7 While everything is steaming, prepare the Kaiser rolls. Cut the rolls in half and put some lettuce on each bottom bun followed by a slice of onion. Smear some mustard (and ketchup and mayo, if desired) on each top bun. Set aside.

8 When 6 minutes are up, uncover the stockpot, lift out the insert with the cheese ramekins (be careful—these will be *hot*), and set aside.

9 Test the doneness of the burgers by gently pressing the top of a patty with the tongs. If the surface gives just a little, it's perfect. If the surface gives a lot, it's undercooked. If it feels like a rock, they're overcooked. But don't worry! You have 4 more patties to get it just right.

10 Once they're fully cooked, use the tongs to transfer the steamed burgers to the prepared Kaiser rolls; pour the hot, molten cheddar over the patties; and close with the top buns. Eat immediately and enjoy, though be careful—the beef will be steaming hot.

NEW JERSEY
THE JERSEY BURGER

New Jersey has made many contributions to the wide world of food. Salt-water taffy, the deep-fried hotdog known as the Ripper, and late night diner snack Disco fries, which are smothered in brown gravy and cheese, to name just a few. Jersey is also known for—but not the originator of—the slider. It is perhaps New Jersey's immense number of working diners that have helped to keep the classic slider tradition alive and well. Places like White Manna in Hackensack and White Rose in Linden still make sliders the way White Castle did in the very beginning. Corporate White Castle today has nothing on the sliders of Manna and Rose, which serves a fresh-beef version that is probably identical to the burgers of 1920s America—small, simple, and addictively tasty.

One of my favorite food items in New Jersey is the cultish Taylor pork roll. This sliceable deli meat, first created by New Jersey senator John Taylor in 1856, actually predates the invention of the burger by half a century. If you order a breakfast sandwich in some parts of Jersey, there's a good chance your egg and cheese will be joined by a slice of cooked Taylor pork. Unctuous and garlicky, Taylor pork is a cross between Spam and bologna but better than both. When pan-fried, the fats render, creating a crazy, salty disk of wow. When added to a burger, watch out. It's hard to put a Jersey burger down.

It was only a matter of time before someone slipped a slice of Taylor pork roll on a burger. One of the best places to experience this treat is at White Rose, the timeless, stainless-steel diner in Linden. Owner Rich

Rich Belfer, White Rose, Linden, New Jersey

Belfer created the Jersey burger in 1999 by marrying a slice of Taylor pork to his "large" slider (basically a slider with twice the meat), which has onions pressed into the patty as it cooks on the flat top. He also has a version of the burger with a fried egg on top that he calls the Jersey Girl.

You could probably use just about any thick-cut, pan-fried deli meat like salami or bologna for your burger, but for the full Jersey experience get your hands on some authentic Taylor pork roll. Make a friend in New Jersey and have them start shipping the stuff. You can thank me later.

THE JERSEY BURGER

MAKES 8 CHEESEBURGERS

EQUIPMENT

A seasoned cast-iron skillet or flat top

A stiff spatula

A mandoline slicer (you can use a sharp knife, but it will be very hard to get the onions thin enough)

A medium-size mixing bowl

A #12 salad scoop

THE BURGER

Beef tallow (rendered beef fat; see page 18)

2 pounds (about 1 kg) fresh-ground 80/20 chuck

2 medium Vidalia or Walla Walla onions, sliced into super-thin rings (translucent and thinner than paper)

Salt, for seasoning

1 (6-ounce) package Taylor pork roll (8 slices)

8 slices yellow American cheese (deli slices, not prepackaged "singles")

8 soft white buns

THE TOPPINGS

This is neither the time nor the place.

1 Preheat the cast-iron skillet over medium heat (or a flat top to medium), and add some beef tallow. Use the spatula to spread the fat, coating the cooking surface.

2 Place the ground beef in the mixing bowl. Using the salad scoop, make balls of beef and gently release them onto the hot pan with 2 to 3 inches (5 to 7 cm) of space surrounding each. Grab a golf ball–size pile of the thin-sliced onion and push it into the center of each ball of beef. Season each ball with salt.

3 Use the stiff spatula to press directly down onto the balls, smashing them into thin, wide patties. Don't worry if you think you've smashed the patties too thin—they'll shrink up to the size of your bun as they cook. The onions should fuse nicely with the raw beef. Once the patties are smashed, don't touch them again until they're ready to flip—5 minutes or until red moisture begins to form on the surface of the patties.

4 Meanwhile, in another part of the pan, heat the Taylor pork roll slices until they're just browned on both sides. You'll need to cut four evenly spaced slits in each slice to prevent them from curling up in the pan (see photo, page 240).

5 Flip the beef-and-onion patties and slide a slice of American cheese on top of each. Cook an additional 2 to 2½ minutes and transfer to the squishy buns.

6 Top with a slice of Taylor ham followed by the top buns and serve immediately.

MASSACHUSETTS

THE HAMBURGER PARM

Although variations of this burger can be found throughout America, it has solid roots in the small Massachusetts town of Fitchburg at a great little lunch counter aptly named The Italian Burger. It's a full-service diner with an extensive menu of home-cooked meals like meatloaf, and fried haddock on Fridays. But of course for me the standout item is their namesake burger.

At Italian Burger a standard griddle-smashed patty of fresh beef is served on a classic loaf of Italian bread (crunchy exterior, pillow-soft interior), slathered in homemade red sauce, and topped with melted provolone cheese. The cheeseburger and meatball hero collide, and the result is pretty spectacular.

Meatballs, which I love as much as the next guy, are not hamburgers. Loaded up with breading, eggs, spices, and often pork instead of beef, meatballs are second cousins to meatloaf. Using a burger patty, pure and simple, allows the beefiness to burst through. Add a simple tomato sauce, great bread, and a slice of melted sharp provolone, and you have yourself one unique American (er, Italian) burger.

It's important to get the right bread and make the tomato sauce at home. My recipe for red sauce (page 245) has evolved over the years. I started eliminating different spices each time I made it; today my pared-down version includes only four ingredients. Easy and delicious.

THE HAMBURGER PARM

MAKES 8 BURGERS

EQUIPMENT

A baking sheet

A stiff spatula

A seasoned cast-iron skillet

A medium-size mixing bowl

A #12 salad scoop

THE TOPPINGS

My Red Sauce (recipe follows)

8 slices sharp provolone

THE BURGER

1 to 2 loaves fresh Italian bread, cut into 8 squares (4 inches/10 cm each) and sliced in half, lengthwise

Beef tallow (rendered beef fat; see page 18)

2 pounds (about 1 kg) fresh-ground 80/20 chuck

Salt, for seasoning

1 Make the red sauce and set it aside, covered, to keep it warm. Preheat the broiler to 500°F (260°C).

2 Place the bread slices, soft side up, on a baking sheet and toast in the broiler (keep an eye on these—they will burn to a crisp if you look away). When they are just golden brown, remove from the oven and set aside.

3 Use the ground chuck to prepare Griddle-Smashed Classic Cheeseburgers (page 32) or Thick Pub Classic Burgers (page 44)—your choice, depending on your mood. Slightly condensed directions for making smashed burgers are repeated here.

4 Preheat the cast-iron skillet over medium heat, add beef tallow, and spread the fat with the spatula to coat the cooking surface.

5 Put the ground chuck in your mixing bowl and use the salad scoop to make slightly heaping balls of beef, placing them on the heated skillet as you go. Each ball should have about 3 inches (7 cm) of space around it. (You may only be able to cook 2 or 3 burgers at a time.)

6 Sprinkle a generous pinch of salt on each ball of beef and then, using your stiff spatula, press them down, *hard*, until you have wide patties just a bit larger than the bread. Let them cook, undisturbed, for 2½ minutes or until reddish liquid begins to form on the surface of the patties.

7. Flip them *once*, don't press them again, and let them cook for another 2 minutes. Meanwhile, prep the bottom half of each piece of toasted bread with a thin layer of red sauce.

8 When the burgers are cooked through, place them on the prepared bread, and add more sauce. Top with a slice of provolone and return the baking sheet to the broiler, removing the top buns from the sheet pan before you do so. When the cheese is melted and gooey, remove the burgers from the broiler, add the top buns, and enjoy.

MY RED SAUCE
Makes enough to top 8 Hamburger Parms

This is a very basic and utilitarian red sauce that has taken me years to perfect. I use it on pizza, for meat sauces, and in any recipe that asks for a red sauce. One cool trick I picked up from an Italian chef friend was to use a blender to fully mix the flavors. It partially emulsifies the oil with the liquid content of the tomatoes, making for a damn tasty sauce.

3 tablespoons (45 ml) olive oil
4 cloves garlic, minced
1 (28 ounce/790 g) can organic whole peeled or diced tomatoes
Sea salt, to taste

1 Heat the oil in a saucepan over medium heat. Add the garlic and stir, cooking until just golden. (Don't burn the garlic, or it will impart a bitter flavor to your sauce.)

2 Add the tomatoes, with their juices, cover, reduce the heat to low, and cook for 10 minutes.

3 Remove from the heat and transfer to a blender. Blend for 3 to 5 seconds (the sauce will become slightly lighter in color) and return to the saucepan. Alternately, puree using an immersion (stick) blender in the saucepan if you have one.

4 Cover the pot and simmer the sauce for another 20 minutes to allow the flavors to incorporate.

THE AMERICAN BURGER, GLOBALLY SPEAKING

The American hamburger saw a meteoric rise in popularity during the 1920s and 1930s, thanks to White Castle and its numerous copycats. That was followed by a postwar, coast-to-coast proliferation in the 1940s, when the burger became associated with car culture, and burger mania grew exponentially. The next obvious step was for America to export this tasty homegrown treat.

In the 1950s small operators like McDonald's and Burger King figured out how to commoditize and franchise their burger businesses into global chains. The first to send its fast-food model overseas was Burger King, in 1963, when the company opened a location in San Juan, Puerto Rico. McDonald's followed in 1967, opening its first location outside the United States in British Columbia, Canada. Today there are more than 39,000 McDonald's and Burger King locations *outside* the States. That is an enormous number of burger restaurants.

The issue with this global expansion was that in order to succeed, these corporations needed to find efficiencies, and the burger became a frozen, desiccated version of its former self. Unfortunately, this was the initial version of the American burger that the world saw—arguably not a great first impression. Regardless, popularity of the American burger soared overseas. Soon after landing in their respective countries, entrepreneurial restaurateurs began to open burger joints that mimicked the American classic with a local spin. The opening of a Burger King or McDonald's spurred folks in the global food community to make burgers that were arguably better, and absolutely different, from the American exports.

Although to some Americans these burgers may seem like inauthentic copies of the real thing, they are in fact beloved locally and without question part of local food culture in many countries. This chapter highlights a few of my favorite examples of burgers that have, over multiple generations and decades, moved from American export to local icon.

It's time to celebrate and appreciate what happened to the American burger as it began to capture the imagination of the world.

THE BØFSANDWICH

This burger is sometimes referred to as the Danish gravy burger for obvious reasons. It may appear to be a stunt burger, but the gravy is actually integral to this burger's history.

Before it migrated from Germany to the United States at the end of the nineteenth century, the Hamburg steak was served on a plate with gravy and slow-cooked soft onions. Today in Germany it's known as a Frikadellen and in Denmark the Hakkebøf. As the story goes, a visiting Dane in the United States in the 1940s fell in love with the American hamburger. This checks out because, at the time, the burger had yet to leave US shores and was experiencing tremendous growth and popularity from coast to coast. The Danish visitor returned home to Copenhagen with tales of tasty burgers and excited Oscar Pettersson, who opened the first burger joint in Denmark in 1949. He and his wife, Anni, opened Oscars Bøf Bar in the world's oldest amusement park, Bakken, just north of Copenhagen. Their version, however, was a cross between the traditional Hakkebøf and an American burger. Today, more than seventy years later, Oscars is still open and serving the same Bøfsandwich.

This is where the story gets odd. For whatever reason, Oscars Bøfsandwich did not take off in Copenhagen in the 1950s. And the version from Oscars bears little resemblance to the gravy-smothered version found in Copenhagen today. I dove deep into the origin story of this burger and eventually came up with answers. I spoke to good friend Klaus Wittrup in Denmark, who runs a successful burger chain in Copenhagen called Gas-

Oscar's Bøf Bar, Klampenborg, Denmark, circa 1955

oline Grill. Klaus is from the Jutland Peninsula, which is essentially rural country similar to the Midwest in the United States. It was in Jutland that the gravy burger proliferated, and here's why: In the early days, most vendors who sold hot dogs had no way of cooking burger patties at their stands. Instead, they would cook burgers at home and bring the precooked patties to their stands. The preferred method of transport was in hot gravy to keep the patties moist: a brilliant solution and an excellent origin story.

In the same way that the lowly hamburger in America made the jump somewhat recently from greasy spoon sustenance to gourmet menu item, the Bøfsandwich witnessed a similar shift in Denmark. About ten years ago chefs in Copenhagen elevated it to knife-and-fork status, increased the size, and started using higher-quality ingredients. The Bøfsandwich is now a massive, hot, wet mess loaded with a few classically Danish ingredients like pickled beetroot, remoulade, and copious "soft onions" (the term Danes use for caramelized onions). Make this one to impress your friends, and remember that it started with one Dane's obsession with the American hamburger.

THE BØFSANDWICH

MAKES 3 BURGERS

EQUIPMENT

A seasoned cast-iron skillet

A 4-inch (10-cm) food ring or round cutter

3 (8-inch/20-cm) parchment paper squares

A stiff spatula or turner

A medium-sized wide saucepan

Metal tongs

THE BURGER

1 pound (about 500 g) fresh-ground 80/20 chuck

4 cups (scant 1L) pork gravy

1 tablespoon butter

3 large sturdy seeded buns

Salt, for seasoning

THE TOPPINGS

Pickled beets, diced

Dijon mustard

Ketchup

Danish Remoulade (recipe follows)

1 medium onion, diced

Sweet bread and butter pickle chips

Caramelized Onions (see recipe, page 54)

Crispy onions (see Fried Onion Hay recipe, page 296)

1 Divide the beef into 3 equal portions (roughly 5.3 ounces/166 g each).

2 Place the food ring on a cutting board or hard surface lined with a parchment square and add a portion of beef. Gently press the beef into the ring to create a perfectly round patty. (I use the ring for consistent thickness, but you can eyeball the size if you prefer. Just be sure not to over-press the meat—you want to maintain a somewhat loose grind.)

3 Remove the ring and set aside. Repeat steps 2 and 3 to form the other 2 patties.

4 Add the pork gravy to a wide saucepan set over low heat, to warm. Don't let it boil, and cover until ready to use.

5 Heat the cast-iron skillet over medium heat and add a pat of butter.

6 Once melted and bubbling, add the buns to the pan, cut-sides down, to toast.

7 Check on them every minute or so and remove them from the pan once they're perfectly golden brown. Set aside.

8 Raise the heat under your skillet to medium-high. Once hot, salt the patties on both sides and place them in pan; they should sizzle loudly when they hit the pan. Cook for 4 to 5 minutes, undisturbed. The goal here is to sear the burgers, sealing in the juices. When you see red liquid start to form on the uncooked surface of the burgers, it's time to flip.

9 Reduce the heat to medium and cook for an additional 4 minutes (again, do not disturb them while cooking).

10 When the patties are done, transfer them to the saucepan full of gravy.

11 The Construction (note: Don't build this burger until you are ready to eat!):
A Place the toasted heel of the bun on a sturdy plate and add some pickled beets.
B Using the tongs, transfer a patty to the bun and begin placing the very specific order of ingredients: first, a small dollop of Dijon mustard, then some ketchup, remoulade, diced raw onion, pickles chips, caramelized onions, and, finally, the toasted crown of the bun.
C Next, pour a healthy dose of the pork gravy over the entire burger and top immediately with a handful of crispy onions.

12 Grab a knife and fork and start eating. Some people will simply pick up the Bøfsandwich to eat it, but if you do you may require a hose-down following lunch (and a nap).

DANISH REMOULADE
Makes enough for 6 burgers

I love mayo-based sauces in all their forms, but those who know me best know that I'm not really a burger sauce guy. Sometimes a sauce can overwhelm the burger, hiding the flavor of the beef and creating a sloppy, hard-to-handle mess.

All around the world chefs use mayonnaise as a base for their secret sauces on burgers. I firmly believe that mayonnaise is the second-best gift to the world by the French (pasteurization being number one) and that if used correctly in a sauce it can elevate the burger experience.

Danish remoulade is one of the greatest sauces out there, and it's predominantly found on smørrebrød, Danish open-faced sandwiches. Naturally, it made its way to the Danish Bøf-sandwich, so you will need to make it for this burger recipe.

½ cup (120 ml) mayonnaise
½ clove garlic, minced
1 teaspoon lemon juice
2 tablespoons Dijon mustard
2 teaspoons prepared horseradish
2 dashes Worcestershire sauce
1 tablespoon finely diced dill pickle or cornichon
½ teaspoon pickle brine
½ teaspoon white sugar

Mix all the ingredients together in a bowl and place in the fridge for at least 30 minutes to rest. This will allow the flavors to mingle.

TURKEY

THE ISLAK

Directly translated, *islak* is the Turkish word for "wet," making this Turkish late-night delight the famous wet burger. There couldn't be a better name for this dish.

It is believed that this burger was invented at the fast-food cafe Kristal Bufe in Istanbul's Taksim Square in the 1970s. A few friends who had visited Istanbul raved about this burger, and Anthony Bourdain included the islak briefly in an episode of *No Reservations* in 2009, saying, "This takes soggy to new extremes. It's quite good." But it was my chef friend Johann Cottier of Frenchette Bakery in New York City who ate a handful of them in Taksim Square, came home, and described for me in vivid detail what they tasted like. I have still not had the real thing in Istanbul, but after endless research, testing, and mouthwatering conversations with Chef Johann, I'm pretty sure we've gotten very close. Regardless, these are some ridiculously tasty burgers.

From what I can tell there is more than one way to make the islak burger, though all methods lead to the same result—a spiced beef burger that is nestled into a soft bun steamed with garlicky sweet tomato sauce. If you can imagine a meatball sub, minus the gooey cheese, and add the flavors of Middle Eastern cuisine, then you are in the zone. In Taksim, the burgers are small, slider-sized, and held in small glass steam boxes until a customer purchases them. They are one of the perfect street burgers—hot, savory, inexpensive, and ready to eat.

What sets this burger apart from all others is the spice added to the raw patty. I'm not usually in favor of adding anything to beef before cooking, because I believe a burger should taste, first and foremost, like beef. In this case I'm prepared to accept this unique interpretation by cooks on the other side of the world. Clearly there is a passionate fanbase for the islak burger in Istanbul, and that version bears only the slightest resemblance to the traditional American burger.

The preparation for the patties for the islak burger is essentially the same as making kofta, one of the meaty hallmarks of Middle Eastern cuisine. All the greatest hits are in there—garlic, cumin, oregano, paprika, black pepper, coriander, and more. Add a soft bun soaked with garlicy tomato sauce and you have a flavor bomb that is both familiar and exotic.

THE ISLAK

MAKES 12 SLIDER-SIZED BURGERS

EQUIPMENT

Mixing bowls, 1 small and 1 large

A small sauté pan

A large well-seasoned cast-iron skillet

A stiff spatula

A stovetop tiered steaming pot

Long metal tongs

A flexible/thin metal spatula

THE BURGER

1 teaspoon salt

1 tablespoon garlic powder

½ teaspoon ground black pepper

½ teaspoon ground cumin

½ teaspoon ground coriander

½ teaspoon dried oregano

¼ teaspoon ground cinnamon

1 teaspoon paprika

1½ pounds (about 750 g) fresh-ground 80/20 chuck

¼ cup (15 g) chopped fresh parsley

½ cup (65 g) grated sweet onion

My Red Sauce (see recipe, page 245, but add 2 extra cloves of garlic)

Neutral oil or beef tallow, for greasing the pan

12 slider-sized buns

1 Start by blending the salt and all of the dry spices in a small bowl.

2 Put the beef into a larger mixing bowl and add the dry spice mixture, parsley, and onion. Work the ingredients into the beef with your (clean) hands until well blended.

3 Divide the beef mixture into 2-ounce (60-g) balls (you can weigh or eyeball here) roughly the size of ping-pong balls, and set aside.

4 Warm the red sauce in a sauté pan over low heat and keep covered on a very low simmer.

5 Next, heat a cast-iron skillet over medium heat and add a bit of oil or beef tallow.

6 When the pan is hot (just beginning to smoke), add a few of the balls, leaving about an inch of space around each. Smash them thin with a stiff spatula. Note: You can also hand-form patties ahead of time, but smashing is much more fun.

7 Cook the patties for about 2 minutes per side and then transfer to the sauce. Once you have all the patties cooked and in the sauce, it's time to steam. You can either leave them there, to luxuriate in the sauce, or assemble the burgers right away.

8 Prepare a steaming pot with about 2 inches (5 cm) of water and bring to a boil to get a good steam going.

9 Use the metal tongs to insert the wet, saucy patties into the split slider buns (if you haven't already) and place them, whole, into the steamer (3 at a time).

10 Smear a dollop of the sauce on top of each bun, cover, and gently steam for about 3 minutes.

11 Use a flexible spatula to remove from the steamer and enjoy. Taste the flavors of Turkey and enjoy a unique interpretation of the American burger at the same time.

THE SLOPPY BURGER

If you like burgers as much as I like burgers, then you already understand that the clearest path to hamburger satisfaction is the harmony of elements. In burger architecture (see page 26), taking into consideration what happens in your mouth upon first bite should be your only concern. I spend far too much time schooling future burger experts on the virtues of simplicity. This burger challenges that notion but keeps form and function in check. So don't be fooled by the name "sloppy"; it is actually a very well-constructed burger made on the street and is spicy as hell. This is Malaysia's famous sloppy burger.

The people of Malaysia love this burger and have given it a few names: the Sloppiest Burger, the Sampah (which is Malaysian for "rubbish")—the most famous is the Ramly Burger. That's because it was invented by a guy named Ramly bin Mokni. In 1979 Ramly started selling his burgers from a street cart in Kuala Lumpur at a time when no one in the country understood or even liked burgers. He experimented with seasoning, hot spice, and wild flavors and in a very short time was a huge success. He expanded and franchised, selling his frozen patties to other street vendors. It is said that today there are tens of thousands of street vendors using Ramly patties in Malaysia.

Every vendor has their own spin on this burger, but there are a few rules you need to follow to make it a true Malaysian street burger. Most vendors use inexpensive ingredients, like margarine instead of butter, and very cheap buns. To be authentic you'll have to do the same. You'll also

Beloved vendor Brader John, Kuala Lumpur, Malaysia

need to find a few special ingredients, namely Malaysian hot sauce (which is fiery hot and sweet), Maggi seasoning (a staple of Southeast Asian cooking), and some Kewpie mayo. And then there's the method: prepare to work for your meal. This is not just a flavor bomb; it's a flavor bomb wrapped in a fried egg.

The marriage of egg and burger is something you rarely see in America, especially in a classic burger joint. Although in the last decade, many high-end restaurants have been elevating their gourmet burgers by topping them with a fried egg. For the other side of the globe, it's a different story. In Australia, order a burger with "the lot" (see page 272) and you'll get, along with many other ingredients, a burger with a fried egg on top. And throughout Southeast Asia the egg plays prominently in the cuisine. The street vendors of Malaysia take things to the next level by wrapping burger patties in a big, wide fried egg (think omelet as thin as a crepe). It's the perfect late-night-drinking food, and if you get the method and the ingredients just right, you'll be transported to the streets of Kuala Lumpur.

THE SLOPPY BURGER

MAKES 4 BURGERS

EQUIPMENT

A seasoned cast-iron skillet

A nonstick pan

A rubber spatula

2 (8-inch/20-cm) parchment paper
   squares

A burger spatula or turner

THE BURGER

1 pound (about 500 g) fresh-ground
   80/20 chuck

Margarine (or butter)

4 classic cheap white hamburger buns

Super-Secret Sloppy Seasoning (recipe
   follows)

4 eggs

4 slices American cheese

Maggi seasoning

Worcestershire sauce

Malaysian hot sauce (or sriracha)

Kewpie mayonnaise

1 Divide the beef into 4 equal portions
(4 ounces/125 g) each.

2 Then, using 2 squares of parchment
paper, hand-smash each portion between
the sheets until they are about ⅛ inch
(3 mm) thick.

3 Heat the skillet over medium heat and
add a good amount of the margarine. Toast
all the buns, insides-down, in batches and
then set aside.

4 Raise the skillet heat to medium-high
and, once starting to smoke, add 2 of the
patties and sprinkle them generously with
the Sloppy Seasoning. Cook for 3 minutes,
or when red condensation begins to form
on the top of the patties.

5 Flip and cook for another minute or so,
then repeat with the other 2 patties.

6 Remove the patties from the heat and
set aside.

7 Heat the nonstick pan over medium heat
and add . . . more margarine.

8 When the pan is decidedly hot, crack an
egg in it and use the rubber spatula break
the yolk and smear it into the egg white.

9 Lift the pan and tilt to coat the surface
with the egg, thinning the egg in the same
way you might make a crepe (if you make
crepes).

10 Turn off the heat and add a slice of
cheese to the center of the egg.

11 Place a cooked patty on the cheese, more seasoning, a dash of Maggi, a dash of the Worcestershire, a squirt of the Malaysian hot sauce, and a squirt of Kewpie.

12 Using the rubber spatula, fold the edges of the egg over the top of the patty. Remove the whole pocket of goodness from the pan, flip over, and place on the toasted heel of the bun (OR place the heel of the bun cut-side down on the burger, remove from the pan, and flip onto a plate). To be true to form (and the name of the recipe) add some MORE hot sauce and mayo, and finally the toasted crown of the bun.

13 Take a bite and be absolutely amazed by the flavors and textures that you will *never* find on a burger in the United States.

SSSS (SUPER-SECRET SLOPPY SEASONING)
Makes enough for 4 Sloppy Burgers

(Shhh . . .)

1 teaspoon classic Indian curry powder
1 teaspoon onion powder
1 teaspoon garlic powder
1 teaspoon paprika
½ teaspoon ground cumin
½ teaspoon ground black pepper
½ teaspoon salt
½ teaspoon white sugar

Combine all the ingredients in a small bowl and blend together with a whisk.

BRAZIL

THE X-TUDO BURGER

In the past ten to fifteen years Brazil has seen massive growth in the popularity of the traditional American hamburger, arguably beginning with one of my favorite spots, the Burger Map, in São Paulo. They used the map in the back of my first book, *Hamburger America*, and created a menu full of regional burgers from the United States and beyond, using fresh ground beef and appealing to a younger generation. Today in Brazil there are thousands of new burger joints popping up everywhere, serving all sorts of American standards, like smashburgers and Oklahoma fried onion burgers, in an attempt to erase the bad taste (pun intended) the McWendyKings had imported decades earlier.

But the burger has always had a quiet presence in Brazil that predates the current renaissance. The classic burger counter Hamburguer do Seu Oswaldo in the Ipiranga neighborhood of São Paulo has been making the same tasty griddled burger served with nothing more than house-made mayo, a mozzarella-type cheese called *queijo prato*, and a simple dollop of crushed tomato since 1966. And then there is the X-Tudo.

I have only seen this late-night burger in Rio, but apparently it's everywhere in the country, served at tiny roadside stands and food carts. I've also consumed them in the Brazilian enclave of Newark, New Jersey, and I'm told they can be found in Brazilian neighborhoods of Florida and Massachusetts.

The X-Tudo has no origin story or credited inventor that we know of, and when you see one you may surmise it simply looks like an attempt to make a bloated American-style hamburger with a distinctly Brazilian twist. Or possibly it's a burger designed to use whatever is on hand in the kitchen to fill the bellies of late-night drunks. Whatever the reason for its existence, this beast makes Brazilians very happy.

The name is a play on words, a combination of Portuguese and English. The letter "X" is pronounced "sheesh" in Portuguese, and *tudo* means "everything." Pronounced in English it sort of sounds like cheese tudo, or cheese everything. Obviously the *tudo* refers to every condiment at the short-order cook's disposal, no matter how bizarre or incongruous.

Depending on where you are in Brazil, the ingredients will change; however, there are a few things that need to be in there to make it an X-Tudo, or Brazilian burger. Following the American burger roadmap, expect the usual suspects like lettuce, tomato, and bacon; then head down the strange burger toppings route and find a laundry list of oddities. Corn, peas, and shredded carrots are fairly common, but I've also seen wacky things like grated Parmesan cheese, raisins, and olives. Potato sticks, a slice of ham, or a sliced hot dog may also be present, and of course cheese. For sauces expect mayo, ketchup, mustard, and beyond.

This is not the sort of burger you will find in a Brazilian steakhouse or fine dining establishment. Even the new wave of burger joints in Brazil have shied away from this street sustenance. You will see the word *podrao* to describe these late-night haunts (with a tongue-in-cheek direct translation of "very rotten"), giving you an idea of the state of mind one will likely be in upon ordering an X-Tudo. The choice to eat this burger, on the street after a night of partying, could be an unhealthy decision, but in Brazil if you are *larica* (have the munchies), a *podrao* is the cure.

THE X-TUDO BURGER

MAKES 3 BURGERS

EQUIPMENT

A 4-inch (10-cm) food ring or round
  cutter

3 (8-inch/20-cm) parchment paper
  squares

A well-seasoned cast-iron skillet

A spatula

A cover to fit the cast-iron skillet
  (a domed lid or metal bowl)

THE BURGER

1 pound (about 500 g) fresh-ground
  80/20 chuck

3 large sturdy seeded buns

Neutral oil or beef tallow, for greasing
  the pan

Salt, for seasoning

THE TOPPINGS

(really, the sky is the limit here,
  but to stay authentic let's make
  a classic version)

Mayonnaise

Ketchup

1 medium beefsteak tomato, sliced

Green-leaf lettuce

Corn (roasted fresh kernels or canned)

6 slices mozzarella cheese

3 slices deli ham

3 fried eggs (see Burger-Perfect Fried
  Eggs, page 292)

Thin-Cut Fried Potatoes (see recipe,
  page 183)

ADDITIONAL TOPPINGS THAT ARE
  ALSO AUTHENTIC

Bacon

A cooked hot dog, split lengthwise

Raisins

Grated carrots

Cooked green peas

Shredded Parmesan cheese

Olives

1 Divide the beef into three equal portions (roughly 5.3 ounces/166 g).

2 Place the food ring on a hard surface lined with a sheet of parchment paper. Fill the ring with a portion of the beef and press to form it into a patty, maintaining a somewhat loose grind. Remove the ring and form the other 2 patties the same way.

3 Prepare all of the toppings you plan to use and have them ready to go.

4 Toast your buns according to the recipe on page 33.

5 On the toasted heel of the bun add some mayo, ketchup, a tomato slice, lettuce, and a handful of the corn.

6 Add a few drops of oil or tallow to the cast-iron skillet, using a spatula to spread it around, and crank it up to medium-high heat. When the pan just starts to smoke, it's ready.

7 At this point, and not before, season both sides of the patties with salt.

8 Place the patties into the hot skillet—they should sizzle loudly when they hit the pan—and cook for 5 minutes without disturbing them. The goal here is to sear the burgers, sealing in the juices. When you see red liquid start to form on the uncooked surface of the burger, it's time to flip them.

9 On the flip add 2 slices of the cheese and a folded slice of ham, reduce the heat to medium, and cover with a large domed lid or small metal bowl.

10 After about a minute, check to see if the cheese has melted. If not, splash a bit of water in the pan, cover again, and wait 10 to 15 seconds.

11 Remove the burgers from heat and allow to rest for 1½ minutes. The internal temperature of the burgers should be about 143°F (62°C) for medium-rare.

12 Now is the time to cook your fried eggs, sunny side up (see recipe, page 292). When finished, remove the pan from the heat.

13 Move the patties to your prepared bottom buns and add the fried egg. The shoestring fries come next, then a swipe of mayo to the inside of the bun, crown, and you are done.

HOW TO MAKE A WAXED PAPER BAG TO HOLD YOUR X-TUDO

The X-Tudo is and should be an unruly mess and almost too much to handle. In Brazil they are served in waxed paper bags in an attempt to keep the thing from imploding or falling apart. To make one at home, simply follow these instructions:

1 Tear a piece of parchment or waxed paper that is roughly square (the same length as the width of a standard roll).

2 Fold in half, and then in half again until you have a smaller square.

3 Find the opening on the cut side (not folded) that will serve as a pocket and insert your X-Tudo.

4 Good luck: This bag will only hold up for a few minutes. Eat fast!

AUSTRALIA

BURGER WITH THE LOT

As far as burgers go, technically this is a stunt burger. The absurd combination of seemingly disparate ingredients tests your willingness to take that first bite; however, this burger has two things most contemporary stunt burgers do not have: history and pride. This burger is, unquestionably, Australia's most famous burger.

I've always been surprised and delighted to see what happens to the American burger when it goes abroad. In every corner of the globe, you can find basic versions of that familiar combination of beef, bun, and cheese. And even if it's not traditional, I can always appreciate a country's riff on the traditional American burger. And let me tell you—this burger is no traditional American burger.

Hamburgers landed in Australia in the early 1930s with Greek immigrants, arriving not from Greece but from the United States. Greeks have been in the burger business in the United States since the beginning, so the story checks out. The first Greeks to arrive in Australia were fond of American burgers, diner counters, and soda parlors. But instead of opening soda parlors, which were huge at the time in America, they opened "milk bars" that featured only milkshakes. The very first was opened by Joachim Tavlaridis in Sydney in 1932; it had no seating and a menu limited to milkshakes. Eventually food was introduced, and the burger was central to the menu. The proliferation of the milk bar spread throughout Australia, and eventually every mom-and-pop corner store became a combination milk bar/tuck shop/chip shop, selling everything from candy to fish and chips.

Today in Australia you mostly find the burger with the lot in the backyards and collective memories of proud Aussies, but also in the fading breed of chip shops across the country.

There's fierce debate about what should be on the burger with the lot. Depending on where you are in Australia, you will find ingredients like grilled pineapple, ketchup, and rashers, and the list goes on. If your lot has less than eight ingredients, something went wrong. Passionate Aussies can all agree on at least *one* of those ingredients—*beetroot*. Yep, without that tasty, earthy red tuber it ain't a burger with the lot.

So, why beets? Some historical accounts suggest the inclusion of beets on a burger started as a joke pulled on American Marines stationed in Australia in the 1950s, a prank that went so far they could never take it back. Or maybe it was a way for Aussies to put their stamp on an American import? Whatever the reason, it's never coming off this burger in Australia.

Okay, so let's break down what you might find on a burger with the lot:

- A sturdy toasted sesame seed bun
- A thick grilled beef patty
- A slice of tomato
- Shredded iceberg lettuce
- Middle rashers or bacon
- A slice of melty white cheddar
- Sautéed onion
- Canned, sliced beets, pickled or, if you are an old-timer, not pickled
- A ring of canned pineapple, grilled
- A fried egg, sunny side up (runny yolk is a must)
- Ketchup (but if you are in Sydney, you may find barbecue sauce instead)

This is a fairly complicated burger to make, because having ALL of your ingredients ready for assembly is critical; timing is everything. You may or may not get it right the first time. Don't worry, I'm here to help.

BURGER WITH THE LOT

MAKES 3 BURGERS

EQUIPMENT

3 (8-inch/20-cm) parchment paper
squares

A 4-inch (10-cm) food ring or round
cutter

Charcoal

A charcoal chimney

A charcoal grill

A grill brush

A long-handled grill spatula/turner

A small, well-seasoned cast-iron pan or
fire-ready nonstick pan

A fireproof glove or good kitchen towel

A medium-sized nonstick skillet

A rubber spatula

THE BURGER

3 hearty seeded buns

1 pound (about 500 g) fresh-ground
80/20 chuck

Salt, for seasoning

3 slices melty, mild cheddar cheese

THE TOPPINGS

3 slices thick-cut bacon, cut in half
(or middle rashers if you can find)

Canned pineapple rings

Butter, for greasing a skillet

3 eggs

½ head iceberg lettuce, shredded

1 medium beefsteak tomato, sliced
into at least 3 slices

1 pickled sliced beet

Caramelized Onions (see recipe,
page 54)

Barbecue sauce (or ketchup for
authenticity)

Note: You have free license to add
more of any ingredient to this burger,
but be warned it may not fit in your
face. A little bit of everything should
be just enough.

1 Divide the beef into 3 equal portions (roughly 5.3 ounces/166 g each).

2 Place the food ring on a cutting board or clean surface lined with parchment paper and add a portion of beef. Gently press the beef into the ring to create a perfectly round patty. (I use the ring for consistent thickness, but you can eyeball the size if you prefer. Just be sure not to over-press the meat—you want it to maintain a somewhat loose grind.)

3 Repeat for the other 2 portions of beef and put the patties in the fridge until you're ready to grill.

4 Using the chimney starter, light the charcoal. When coals are ready, transfer them to the grill, making sure that the bottom vent is open. Spread the coals out, leaving space on one side (as a cooler rest spot in case things get too hot in there).

5 Place the grate over the coals and, using a grill brush, scrape off any residual buildup. Cover the grill and make sure that the top vent is wide open.

6 Place your cast iron skillet on the grill and give it some time to heat up. Meanwhile, grab a plate and line it with some paper towels to keep near the grill.

7 Add the bacon to the hot skillet and slide to the cool side of the grill if it gets too hot.

8 Place all of the bun halves cut-side down over the cooler side of the grill and watch them closely—it may only take about a minute to toast them. Use your grill spatula to remove.

9 After a few minutes, flip the bacon and cook until done.

10 Remove the bacon from the heat and transfer to your nearby paper towel–lined plate. Set aside. Use the spatula (or pull out those fire-safe gloves your cool uncle gave you last year) to slide the pan over and out of the way.

11 Next, toss the 3 pineapple rings onto the grill and cook for 20 seconds per side. You are looking to sear, not cook, the pineapple. Use your grill spatula to remove and set aside with the bacon.

12 Let the grill heat up again until your grill grate is ridiculously hot.

13 At this point, and not before, season both sides of your patties with the salt.

14 Place the patties on the hot grill, cover, and leave them alone. Allow the patties to cook for about 3 minutes. The cooking time can vary depending on environmental and equipment factors, so you'll have to use your best judgment here. A good visual cue is when you see red liquid start to form on the uncooked surface of the burger; then it's time to flip. Take a peek just shy of that 3-minute mark.

15 Flip the patties and cook (again, untouched and covered) for an additional 2 minutes, but at about the 1-minute mark, quickly add the sliced cheese and close the grill again, to melt.

16 Transfer the cooked patties to a plate.

17 Carefully wipe most of the bacon grease out of the small, well-seasoned cast-iron pan with some paper towels and add a pat of butter.

18 When the pan is hot and the butter is melted and bubbling, crack the eggs into the pan (all 3 if they'll fit!) and cook until the whites are cooked through but the yolks are still bright and runny.

19 Meanwhile, assemble the rest of your burgers following this handy guide:
A toasted bun heel (bottom)
B shredded iceberg lettuce
C tomato slice
D beetroot
E bacon
F caramelized onion
G grilled pineapple
H patty with cheese

20 The moment your eggs are fried to perfection, add 1 to each burger.

21 Smear the inside of each toasted bun crown (top) with barbecue sauce or ketchup and top to finish.

TOPPINGS
&
SAUCES

STEVE'S COUNTRY-FRIED BACON

MAKES ABOUT 10 PIECES

It is well known that Texans do not shy away from a deep fryer. At the State Fair of Texas every fall, vendors compete for the next great deep-fried treat, and the sky's the limit. One year, deep-fried butter won the prize (butter!), and another it was the year of the deep-fried buffalo chicken in a flapjack. Hundreds have competed, and the ideas continue to amaze. In 2008, though, the top honors at Big Tex went to the somewhat tame chicken-fried bacon—a simple yet brilliant idea for sure.

A few years ago, while I was making the rounds in the Houston area for burgers featured in my state-by-state guidebook *Hamburger America*, I stopped in to visit good friend Steve Christian, then owner of Christian's Tailgate Bar & Grill, a roadhouse on the west side of Houston. Steve is as much a third-generation burger man as a top-notch salesman and innovator. "You need to try my latest creation," he told me excitedly, and that's when I had my first country-fried bacon cheeseburger.

Steve noticed once that a big seller at the Houston rodeo was the country-fried bacon on a stick. "I immediately thought, why not on a hamburger?!" And the rest you can figure out. Like everything in Steve's world, there always has to be a "best" way to make it. So, after much experimenting he settled on a successful formula. The following recipe is directly from Steve.

After you've deep-fried bacon you come to the realization that you really can deep-fry just about anything. Channel your inner State Fair of Texas and get creative.

EQUIPMENT

A deep skillet for frying

Two small or medium mixing bowls

Long tongs (skip the plastic tips!)

INGREDIENTS

Enough peanut oil (or other neutral oil) to fill the skillet with about 2 inches (5 cm) of oil

1 quart (about 1 L) buttermilk

1½ cups (290 g) all-purpose flour

A few shakes of coarse-ground black pepper

¼ cup plus 1 tablespoon (75 g) Lawry's seasoned salt (or make your own version! see recipe below)

1 (16-ounce/455-g) package high-quality, store-bought, thin-sliced bacon

---

SEASONED SALT SUBSTITUTE
Makes ¼ cup plus 1 tablespoon/75 g

---

2 teaspoons ground turmeric
2 teaspoons salt
2 teaspoons onion powder
2 teaspoons garlic powder
2 teaspoons paprika
2 teaspoons sugar

Whisk all the ingredients together and use instead of Lawry's in your dredging flour.

---

1 Heat the oil in a deep skillet over medium heat.

2 In one mixing bowl, add enough buttermilk to submerge a slice of bacon, about 2 cups (480 ml).

3 In a separate bowl, combine the flour, black pepper, and seasoned salt and whisk until blended.

4 When the oil is hot, coat a slice of bacon in the flour mixture, submerge it in the buttermilk, then dredge it through the flour mixture again. Gently drop the battered bacon into the hot oil and cook until golden brown, about 2 minutes. Steve says, "Remember to flip it at least once!" Do not crowd the pan—fry the bacon in 2- or 3-slice shifts.

5 When the bacon is golden and crispy, remove it from the oil, drain briefly on paper towels, and serve on a burger immediately.

Note: The country-fried bacon cheeseburger is a classic Texas two-fister with cheese, lettuce, tomato, onion, pickle, jalapeño, and 1 or 2 slices of fried bacon on top. Country-fried bacon also makes a crazy-good snack, and if you have some pickle chips on hand, I highly recommend frying them, too, while you're at it.

BEANLESS BEEF CHILI SAUCE

MAKES ENOUGH TO TOP 8 BURGERS

Beef chili sauce as a condiment was created out of frugality. Burger joints that use fresh ground beef are often left with a daily dilemma: what to do with unused beef at the end of the day. Beef chili is the perfect solution because it can be refrigerated for up to a week or kept in the freezer for six months. And it tastes great on a cheeseburger.

The history of the chili-topped burger is not well documented, but all roads seem to lead to Los Angeles, California, where arguably it was invented. It was there in the 1920s at the twenty-four-hour chili parlor Ptomaine Tommy's that Thomas DeForest first ladled chili on a burger. His chili burger was imitated by others all over Los Angeles, and one of the best known is the popular chili burger chain Original Tommy's (no relation to Ptomaine Tommy). Today the chili cheeseburger is ubiquitous. Some of the best can be found at Washington, D.C.'s Ben's Chili Bowl, Brooks' Sandwich House in Charlotte, North Carolina, and Marty's Hamburger Stand in Los Angeles.

The chili you'll find at most burger joints is a beanless chili con carne. It's similar to Coney sauce (the sweet chili sauce that adorns many hot dogs in America) but spicier and more tomatoey. If you've never made a chili sauce (or chili for that matter), this recipe is a great place to start. It's a beanless version of my mother's award-winning Mama's Kiss-Ass Chili, the jumping-off point for the great chili cooks my brothers and sisters have become. All of our chilis are different from Mom's in some respect. Mine is no exception.

EQUIPMENT

A large saucepan with a lid

A wooden spoon or spatula

INGREDIENTS

2 tablespoons olive oil

1 medium yellow onion, finely chopped

3 cloves garlic, minced

1 pound (about 500 g) fresh-ground 80/20 chuck

2 pinches salt

1 tablespoon brown sugar

1 tablespoon chili powder

½ teaspoon cumin

1 teaspoon Worcestershire sauce

1 cup (240 ml) canned crushed tomatoes

1 tablespoon tomato paste

1 tablespoon Frank's RedHot cayenne pepper sauce or similar hot sauce

1 Heat the oil in a large saucepan over medium heat.

2 Cook the onion, stirring frequently, until translucent. Add the garlic, cook for 1 minute or until golden, then add the ground beef. Crumble, chop, and stir the beef until browned and pebbly. Scoop off any visible fat with a spoon.

3 Reduce the heat to medium-low and mix in the salt, brown sugar, chili powder, cumin, and Worcestershire.

4 Add the crushed tomatoes, tomato paste, and hot sauce to the pan. Stir to combine.

5 Add ½ cup (120 ml) water, cover the pan, and simmer for 15 minutes. The chili sauce should be thick but not clumpy. Add more water to thin if needed.

GOOP SAUCE

MAKES ENOUGH FOR
12 QUARTER-POUND BURGERS

Goop is a sauce that has made its way onto many burgers in the Pacific Northwest, especially the older-style classic burgers. All of the Goop I've had tastes pretty much the same, and all of the recipes are protected by their respective burger institutions and contain highly secret ingredients. But to legitimately call your sauce Goop, you need to be Chuck Fritsch at Eastside Big Tom in Olympia, Washington. That's because Chuck has trade-marked the name and arguably makes some of the best Goop in the area.

I can see why he keeps his recipe under wraps—Goop is addictive. It adorns not only the burgers at Big Tom but the fries and tater tots as well (tots + Goop = heaven). I once asked Chuck for the recipe, and he said, "What's the saying? If I told you I'd have to kill you?" So he didn't give me the recipe. But I've done some testing and I think I've come pretty close. When I wrote this up years ago I read it back to myself and imagined Chuck laughing.

INGREDIENTS

½ cup (120 ml) mayonnaise

¼ cup (60 ml) sour cream

2 tablespoons sweet relish

3 tablespoons (45 ml) yellow mustard

1 Whisk the mayonnaise, sour cream, relish, and mustard in a bowl and serve on your favorite burgers. The color should resemble a 1971 Curious Yellow Plymouth Barracuda.

2 Tell your friends it's not the real thing but pretty damn close.

HARRY'S SCHNÄCK SAUCE

MAKES ENOUGH FOR 8 QUARTER-POUND BURGERS

Just about every burger joint in America proudly boasts that their signature burger comes with a "special" or "secret" sauce. Most of us who care to investigate cooking secrets have easily picked the lock on the standard special sauce—the Thousand Island knockoff, a ketchup/mustard/mayo combo with a few other uncomplicated ingredients in there for uniqueness. But there's a reason why "special" sauce is actually ubiquitous—this simple combination of flavors can perfectly enhance a beefy burger, so long as the chef goes easy on the ketchup.

Then one day I came across Schnäck Sauce. This is not your typical special sauce. It is robust and spicy without taking away from the flavor profile of beef. It is about as sophisticated a topping as you will find on one of my burgers, and if you like spicy, hot, creamy things, this sauce is for you.

It was developed by my friend Harry Hawk for his burger joint Schnäck, which served sliders he called "schnäckies" in Brooklyn from 2001 to 2007. It really could be one of the best burger sauces out there.

INGREDIENTS

⅓ cup (75 ml) mayonnaise

2 tablespoons grainy mustard

2 small canned Mexican chipotle chiles
(I use La Morena or La Costeña chipotles
in adobo), or more to taste

Salt, for seasoning

1 Combine the mayonnaise, mustard, chiles, and salt to taste in a food processor and pulse until the chiles are blended, about 45 seconds. If it's not spicy enough, add more chiles. If it's too spicy, start over with fewer chiles.

2 Serve on a burger with nothing else. Your taste buds will explode.

PICKLED JALAPEÑOS

MAKES ENOUGH TO FILL A 1-QUART (1-L) JAR

My friend Steve Christian, former owner of Christian's Tailgate Bar & Grill in Houston, Texas, made one of the best jalapeño cheeseburgers in the land. That's because his sliced, pickled jalapeños are incredible, and this makes all the difference. Steve buys them cold-packed from Cajun Chef. He told me once, "This is the only brand that has any crunch," which is true, so you'll need to buy them in large quantities from Steve's supplier, or make your own.

The versatile pickled jalapeño is a staple on just about any roadhouse menu in the great state of Texas. When pickled, jalapeños impart a mellow heat (especially if you remove the seeds) that is not hot enough to damage your taste buds. Fear not, you'll still get a buzz, a sort of mini-high that will naturally elevate your Texas two-fisted burger experience.

EQUIPMENT

A medium saucepan

1-quart (1-L) Mason jar with airtight lid

INGREDIENTS

2 cups (480 ml) distilled white vinegar

2 tablespoons sugar

2 tablespoons salt

8 to 10 cloves garlic, halved lengthwise

12 to 14 medium-size green jalapeños

1 Add 1½ cups (360 ml) water, the vinegar, sugar, and salt to a saucepan and bring to a gentle boil for 1 minute, then remove from the heat and let cool. (I usually put the saucepan in the freezer or fridge for a few minutes, or outside if it's cold, to speed things up.)

2 Place a third of the garlic pieces in the bottom of the Mason jar.

3 Slice the jalapeños into thin rings (don't remove the seeds) and add them to the jar as well, alternating with handfuls of the remaining garlic. Jalapeños can be very hot. Avoid the dreaded capsaicin burn by wearing rubber gloves, and avoid touching your eyes (ouch).

4 Pour the cooled vinegar mixture over the jalapeños, seal the jar tightly, and place in the fridge at least overnight before using them. The best flavor comes out at about day three, and hits its stride by day seven, but the pickles will last in the fridge for months.

5 Remove the seeded centers from the jalapeños before serving to temper the heat. Apply to burgers, deviled eggs (page 316), or just about anything that needs a kick in the flavor.

BURGER-PERFECT FRIED EGGS

MAKES ENOUGH FOR 4 BURGERS

If you like burgers as much as I like burgers then you already understand that the clearest path to hamburger satisfaction is finding a harmony of elements. In considering burger architecture (see page 26), the synthesis that will occur in your mouth upon your first bite should be your only concern. And if that first bite contains a beef patty, cheese, and a fried egg, you may have achieved perfect burger harmony.

The marriage of egg to burger is not something you see all over America, but recently many high-end restaurants are elevating their gourmet burgers by topping them with a fried egg. In Australia, order a burger with "the lot" and you'll get, among other things, a burger with bacon, pickled beetroot, a fried egg, and sometimes pineapple (clearly the creation of late-night drunks). In parts of Southeast Asia the egg is also a prominent burger topping. Street vendors in Kuala Lumpur take things to the next level by wrapping burger patties in big, wide fried eggs for a treat known as the Sloppy (or Ramly) Burger (page 260).

How you prepare an egg for a burger depends on your preference. A scrambled egg has very different taste properties than a fried egg. But, in my mind, nothing says "I don't like you" more than an overcooked egg. The perfectly cooked egg, sunny-side up with a runny yolk, creates nature's perfect burger sauce. The combination of egg yolk and burger grease is a protein-rich sensory explosion.

And the circular shape of a fried egg fits perfectly on a burger. It's as if the partnership were meant to be.

EQUIPMENT

A nonstick skillet for frying eggs

A spatula

INGREDIENTS

2 tablespoons butter (at least ½ tablespoon per egg)

4 large eggs

1 Make classic pub burgers with American or cheddar cheese following the recipe on page 44. While the burger patties are resting, heat butter in a nonstick skillet over medium-high heat. Use enough butter for the number of eggs you're cooking—depending on the size of your skillet, you may be able to cook 2 or 3 at a time.

2 When the butter is hot and just starting to brown, crack the eggs in the pan. Leave enough space between them for the whites to spread out.

3 Cook, untouched, until the whites are just opaque and the yolk is still runny.

4 Angling the pan, gently slide each egg out of the skillet and onto each cooked patty. Serve immediately on toasted buns.

BACON IN THE ROUND

MAKES 1 POUND OF BACON,
OR HOWEVER MUCH YOU NEED

On its own, bacon is heaven. It's the gateway meat for most vegetarians who slip and fall off their diets. And for carnivores it's a drug with a powerful aroma that is virtually impossible to resist. No matter what you are doing, or how full you are, *there is always room for bacon*. Am I wrong?

That said, I'll be totally honest here. Although I understand the popularity of bacon on a burger, I'm not really a fan of it as a topping. Bacon has a very strong flavor that can easily overwhelm the subtle flavors of good beef. However, used sparingly, it can work with your burger, not against it.

Bacon has three distinct flavors: salt, smoke, and fat. Any burger can benefit from the addition of these elements. Cheese also contains salt, and often so does your burger when you add it during the cooking process. That adds up to a lot of salt. Use cheddar instead of American where bacon is involved (cheddar contains half the sodium) and a bit less salt when you season your patties. Generally speaking, the more bacon you use the less you will be able to taste the beef. For best results I recommend using good bacon, but avoid thick-cut bacon from your butcher or slabs of pork belly.

One day during a cooking session in the Hamburger America Test Kitchen we accidentally stumbled upon a new method for preparing bacon as a burger topping. For years I had simply cooked bacon in a pan and placed the cooked planks across the top of a burger, complete with long bits sticking out from under the bun. It never looked right and always seemed clumsy. Then it struck me: What if we cooked the bacon in a *circle* to match the shape of the burger? The result was genius, the method everlasting.

A seasoned cast-iron skillet

Long tongs (skip the plastic tips!)

1 (16-ounce/455 g) package good-quality store-bought bacon, preferably uncured and standard thickness

1 Preheat a cast-iron skillet over medium heat.

2 Using tongs, twirl a strip of raw bacon into a tight, more-or-less flat spiral, making sure the edges are overlapping slightly. Add as many of these bacon spirals as you can fit in the pan with space between them. Cook them *slowly*. If the pan starts to smoke, lower the heat.

3 When your bacon discs are browned on one side, flip gently and cook the other side until they've reached your desired crispiness.

4 Save the rendered pork fat (lard) for other recipes like the San Antonio Bean-burger (page 172). It will keep in the freezer for months.

FRIED ONION HAY

MAKES 2 CUPS (450 G) OR *ALMOST* ENOUGH TO SHARE

This is what I do with leftover onions from my onion burger. And I make a lot of Oklahoma Fried-Onion Burgers (see recipe, page 154). In 2021 alone, I made more than fifteen thousand of them at pop-ups all over America, and I plan to make ten times that with the opening of my new restaurant. For a single event where I may make up to four hundred fried onion burgers, I'll need sixty pounds of onions. That's a lot of onions.

Usually there are leftover thin-sliced sweet onions, and I often struggle to toss them out. I use onions in just about everything I cook, and while I attempt to incorporate the extra supply into other recipes, a lot ends up going to waste. Then I remembered the glorious fried onion strings at the Palm Restaurant and realized my leftover sliced sweet onions had a higher cause.

The Palm did not invent this tasty side dish; French fried onions go back to the nineteenth century and can be found incorporated into dishes around the world. The crispy, thin fried onion is a critical element in Middle Eastern cuisine, is served on every Scandinavian hot dog from Stockholm to Reykjavik, and can be found topping holiday casseroles in the American South. For the latter, canned fried onions are the default, but if you want to truly elevate your casserole game, use these instead.

Deep-frying is an art, but follow some basic rules and you'll be a success: 1) Your onions should be as thin as paper (*cheveux d'ange*, or angel's hair, as the French say). 2) Your flour should be seasoned. And 3) Your oil temperature must be just right. These are the keys to unlocking restaurant-quality fried onion hay.

It makes a great side dish or a topping, piled high on a thick, juicy cheeseburger (just like they do at two of my hometown burger joints: The Good Steer and Triangle Pub on Long Island, New York). You really can't go wrong with crispy fried onions.

EQUIPMENT

A flour sifter, fine sieve, or whisk

A large mixing bowl

A mandoline or deli slicer

A deep cast-iron pan for frying

A probe thermometer

A sheet pan

Paper towels or newspaper

A pair of metal tongs

INGREDIENTS

1 cup (120 g) all-purpose flour

1 tablespoon seasoned salt (see recipe, page 281)

2 medium onions

Canola or grapeseed oil, for frying

1 Sift the flour and seasoned salt together into a large mixing bowl (or use a whisk to incorporate).

2 Slice the onions into the thinnest rings possible using either a mandoline (watch those fingertips!) or a deli slicer. I own a very sturdy home model because we slice so many onions for pop-up events. The onions will produce juice, so you'll need to dry them as best you can with paper towels. You should have about 2 cups (104 g).

3 Add oil to the cast-iron pan, just to the halfway point (and not higher!) to avoid an oil overflow while frying. Over medium heat, bring the oil to around 375°F (190°C) but not more than 400°F (205°C).

4 While the oil is heating, prepare a sheet pan lined with paper towels or newspaper and keep nearby.

5 Working in batches, grab a handful of the onions and dredge in the flour mixture. Shake off as much excess flour as possible, and gently drop the onions into the hot oil. As you drop, use your fingers to separate the onions so they don't clump together. Use a pair of tongs to manipulate and gently turn the onions, cooking until they are golden brown. Keep a close eye on the pan because they will go from perfect to over-cooked in a snap.

6 Transfer the fried onions to your paper towel–lined sheet pan to drain.

7 Consume immediately.

CHEESEBURGER STUFFING

MAKES 8 TO 10 PORTIONS

I know what you are thinking: This sounds silly. Well, hear me out. You are about to make the greatest stuffing, or "dressing" as it's called down South: cheeseburger stuffing. You heard that right. Stuffing is, really, just a deconstructed hamburger with tasty herbs. Think about it: the bread, the meat, the onions, the butter . . . these are some of the hallmarks of a great burger. Add the traditional stuffing herbs and there you have it, a new Thanksgiving recipe to wow the family. You can thank me later.

For this stuffing, I'm using cubed burger buns instead of sliced bread, and ground beef instead of the traditional sausage. I've also added a tiny bit of shredded cheddar cheese at the end to complete the dish.

So why is it called stuffing? If you go all the way back to the Roman Empire, and just about anywhere in the Fertile Crescent at the time, it was common practice to stuff the empty cavity of an animal with another smaller animal before cooking over a fire. Then Roman chef Apicius published a cookbook outlining a stuffing recipe that included nuts, vegetables, brains, and livers. The idea of course was that the stuffing would cook right along with the animal (think: centuries-old one-pot cooking).

The tradition of stuffing a turkey for Thanksgiving came much later, in the early 1800s, with written recipes that are very close to the classic bread-plus-herbs version that we all know so well. At some point in culinary history stuffing and dressing moved from the cavity of the turkey to a casserole dish, cooked separately. There is some scientific reasoning behind this move, and I'm constantly being asked the question: To stuff, or not to stuff?

Stuffing a turkey can be dangerous. A turkey is cooked when the internal temperature reaches 165°F. But at that temperature, you run the risk of *undercooking* your stuffing to cook a perfect bird. If you try to compensate and cook the stuffing correctly, you will very likely overcook and dry out your turkey. There's also the dangerous bacteria part of the science—if the bird is undercooked, the introduction of bacteria is likely. My advice is to just cook the stuffing separately, in a casserole dish in the oven.

My tasty stuffing recipe will seem familiar, not just because of the herb profile and butter, but because it also tastes like a burger. The herb list is what I like to call the Full Simon & Garfunkel because, to make it taste like stuffing, you need dried parsley, sage, rosemary, and thyme. Then you can go to Scarborough Fair.

Time to be a Thanksgiving hero and make this stuffing. But don't limit yourself to the holidays—this recipe is so good you need to make it all year round.

EQUIPMENT

A large baking sheet pan

A large cast-iron skillet

A casserole dish

A large mixing bowl

A large spoon or rubber spatula

INGREDIENTS

1 (8-pack) sandwich potato rolls

**1 pound (about 500 g) fresh-ground
80/20 chuck**

½ cup (1 stick/112 g) salted butter

2 large stalks celery, diced

1 medium white or sweet onion, diced

2 cloves garlic, pressed

1 teaspoon dried parsley

1 teaspoon dried sage

1 teaspoon dried rosemary

1 teaspoon dried thyme

1½ cups (360 ml) beef broth

2 eggs, beaten

**½ cup (57 g) shredded cheddar cheese,
or more to taste**

Optional: Top with beef gravy (see Super-Easy
Tasty Brown Gravy, page 121) to truly enhance
this stuffing.

1 Preheat the oven to 300°F (150°C).

2 Cut the burger buns into crouton-sized cubes and place them on a sheet pan. Bake for 20 minutes, or until they are stiff and dried out, not toasted.

3 Once the buns are done, raise the oven temperature to 350°F (175°C).

4 Next, heat a large skillet over medium heat. Add the beef, chop, and stir, cooking until crumbly and there's no pink in sight. Remove the skillet from heat and drain most of the fat by tilting the pan and scooping out the excess liquid. Discard this (or save for future burgers!).

5 In the same skillet, melt the butter and add the diced celery and onion. Sauté until the onion is translucent, about 5 minutes, then add the pressed garlic and cook for 1 minute more.

6 Add the parsley, sage, rosemary, and thyme and stir to incorporate, then add the beef broth. Cook for 1 minute and then remove from heat.

7 Grease a casserole dish with butter.

8 In a large bowl, mix the eaggs and burger bun croutons together, then immediately add the onion/broth mixture and the cooked ground beef. Stir to incorporate and then dump into the casserole dish.

9 Top with the cheese and bake uncovered for about 35 minutes, until the top is golden brown.

THE WHITE SAUCE

MAKES ENOUGH FOR 6 BURGERS

Those who know me know I don't really like a saucy burger. I like a beefy burger. Sauces can be great, but there is a tendency for heavy-handed burger lovers to over-sauce a burger and completely destroy the flavor/texture harmony that you are trying to achieve. A good sauce is well balanced, simple, and used sparingly. How much sauce should you use on your burger? Start light and experiment—you will find your way.

You also won't find many sauce recipes in this book because most are pretty underwhelming. I truly believe that grease should be considered a condiment, the best natural component to a great burger. That said, this sauce is a winner in my mind. It ticks all the boxes to flavor greatness with only four ingredients and can be used on just about anything you can dream up, including burgers.

This sauce comes from the now-closed New York City gyro sandwich emporium Gyro II. When they closed, I was very sad. But in a strange twist that made the parting bearable, the owners put the recipe for their famous white sauce in the window along with a farewell note. This is the sauce they used on their gyro sandwiches in place of the traditional tzatziki.

Where tzatziki has cucumbers, garlic, and yogurt, this sauce, which they used for forty-five years at Gyro II, was made with mayonnaise, distilled white vinegar, dry dill, and sugar. That's all. The reason for the move away from traditional tzatziki was the garlic. I had the great honor of meeting the man who opened Gyro II in 1972, Richard Feldman, and he explained: the Greek gyro (pronounced YE-RO) was a super-popular lunch option for midtown Manhattan office workers in the early seventies. After about a year of being open they noticed a drop in sales and attributed it to customers not wanting to go back to the office reeking of garlic. Someone suggested this sauce, which came from a recipe for lamb. Once they implemented the new sauce sales started booming and they never looked back.

INGREDIENTS

1 cup (240 ml) mayonnaise (preferably Admiration mayonnaise, but any good mayo will do)

¼ cup (60 ml) distilled white vinegar

1 tablespoon white sugar

1½ teaspoons dried dill (fresh will not work)

Mix all the ingredients together, cover, and place in the fridge for at least 2 hours for the sugar to dissolve and the dill to bloom. That's it! It will last for up to 2 weeks in the fridge. It's a pure science project that works. You can use it on anything. Dip your fries in it, put it on a salad . . . and absolutely put it on a burger. Make this sauce and keep history alive.

Infamous window note, Herald Square, New York City, 2017

SIDES

DEPRESSION-ERA COLE SLAW

MAKES 8 TO 10 SIDE-DISH SERVINGS

If you've ever had the pleasure of eating one of the greatest green chile cheeseburgers in America (at the Santa Fe Bite in New Mexico), then you've probably also had Bonnie Eckre's addictive coleslaw as a side. The recipe she has used for decades is actually adapted from a government-issued pamphlet to help homemakers stretch their grocery dollars during the Great Depression. It was designed to be made with readily available and inexpensive ingredients (in this case, no cream).

INGREDIENTS

1 head white cabbage, shredded

1 green bell pepper, seeded and finely chopped

½ cup (100 g) sugar

⅔ cup (165 ml) distilled white vinegar

¼ cup (60 ml) canola oil

¼ teaspoon salt

½ teaspoon ground black pepper

½ teaspoon celery seed

1 teaspoon ground mustard

1 Place the shredded cabbage and chopped pepper in a large bowl. Pour the sugar over the cabbage and pepper.

2 In a small saucepan, bring the vinegar, oil, salt, black pepper, celery seed, and mustard to a boil. The smell of this boiling concoction will probably drive you out of the kitchen—hang in there. Boil for 5 minutes and then pour the hot brew over the cabbage and peppers. Don't stir it yet! Allow it to cool before stirring. It will appear as if there isn't nearly enough liquid to transform all that cabbage into the saucy coleslaw of your dreams, but trust me, it'll work.

3 When the bowl of slaw and dressing has cooled, mix the contents, cover, and refrigerate for at least 2 hours. Bonnie suggests allowing the slaw to marinate overnight for optimum flavor.

STUPID-EASY COLE SLAW

MAKES ENOUGH FOR A
HUNGRY BACKYARD PARTY OF 8 TO 10

If you don't have time for Bonnie's Depression-Era Cole Slaw, here's one that I came up with years ago that is easy and very tasty. It's your classic, creamy coleslaw; the one you'll find at any good backyard picnic, diner, or seafood shack. It's always a crowd pleaser and, I like to think, a great replacement for a green salad if your guests are clambering for something moderately healthy. And for those who have cringed at slaw recipes that call for buckets of sugar, you'll find none here. Zero. That's because I reformulated the recipe so that a diabetic friend could safely enjoy my coleslaw.

EQUIPMENT

A large mixing bowl
A food processor with a grating/ shredding attachment

INGREDIENTS

1 head white cabbage, shredded
6 medium-large carrots, grated
1 cup (240 ml) mayonnaise
¼ cup (60 ml) apple cider vinegar
2 tablespoons yellow mustard
1 teaspoon salt
½ teaspoon ground black pepper

1 Combine the cabbage and carrots in a bowl and set aside.

2 In the large bowl, whisk together the mayonnaise, vinegar, mustard, salt, and pepper. Add the carrots and cabbage to the mixture, tossing to coat.

3 This slaw can be served immediately, but tastes best if covered and stored in the fridge for an hour before serving. (It can also be made ahead and stored in the fridge for up to 24 hours.)

MAMA'S POTATO SALAD

MAKES 8 TO 10 SIDE-DISH SERVINGS

I've been referring to my mother as "Mama" since I could speak. And my grandmother was her Mama. So although this comes from my mother's enormous cache of recipes, it really belongs to my grandmother, "Granny," the original Mama.

Granny was an incredible Southern home cook. Fried chicken and mac 'n' cheese were her go-to meals, but where she excelled was in good old Lowcountry classics like chicken perlo, shrimp and grits, and sweet tea.

Granny has since passed, so it's my mother who makes the potato salad for gatherings with immediate family. But when the entire Southern family is getting together it's my aunt Brenda who takes the reins. "I'm the only one who really knows how to make it," she's told my mom. "I can make it taste just like Granny's."

It's the boiled egg that makes it taste like Granny's, a staple in any classic potato salad recipe. Somehow eggs have started to fall out of favor in newer potato salad recipes, and I find that puzzling. It's the creamy, rich egg component that unquestionably ties this salad together.

As we were going over the recipe one day Aunt Brenda said, "I don't think Mama put that much onion in there." Balance is key, Brenda warned me. "Not too much of anything that has a flavor of its own." You may need to experiment a bit to get it just right.

INGREDIENTS

3 to 4 pounds (about 1½ to 2 kg) white potatoes, washed, peeled, and cubed

3 large eggs

1 bunch scallions, chopped

½ medium red onion, chopped

3 to 4 stalks celery, finely chopped

½ large green bell pepper, seeded and chopped

½ large red bell pepper, seeded and chopped

½ large yellow bell pepper, seeded and chopped

¾ pint to 1 pint (430 to 480 ml) mayonnaise (I suggest Hellmann's)

2 tablespoons chopped dill pickle or relish

Sea salt, to taste

Paprika, for sprinkling

1 Boil the potatoes in salted water until the potatoes are tender. Drain and set aside.

2 Hard-boil eggs using my Deviled Eggs With a Kick recipe on page 316, cool, and peel. Or follow Granny's method and add the eggs to the boiling water with the potatoes.

3 Transfer the potatoes to a large bowl and add the chopped scallions; celery; the green, red, and yellow peppers; and the eggs. Add half the mayonnaise to the bowl and the chopped pickle. Using a spoon, combine gently. Add the remaining mayonnaise as you stir.

4 Chill for at least an hour and serve. Give the bowl a sprinkle of paprika just before serving.

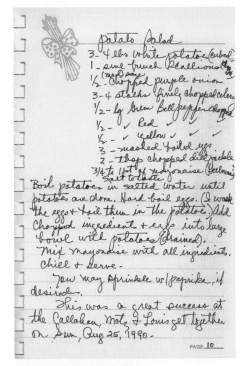

A page from Granny's recipe book

RED CHILE POTATO CHIPS

MAKES 8 TO 10 SIDE-DISH SERVINGS

Anyone can walk into a grocery store and buy a bag of chips. The potato chip is the most popular savory snack out there, making up about 25 percent of all snacks consumed worldwide. The flavor choices beyond salt are also seemingly unlimited these days. Potato chips are really easy to make, so when you have the option to fry a batch of chips at home, go for it.

If I'm deep-frying food at home, I always think about alternate uses for the fry oil before I toss it—this is a great opportunity to make your own potato chips. They're fast, easy, tasty, and you can flavor them any way you like. Try a version with just salt or, my favorite, a sprinkle of red chile powder and salt.

EQUIPMENT

A seasoned cast-iron skillet

A mandoline slicer or a sharp knife and a steady hand

A slotted spoon or mesh straining spoon

INGREDIENTS

3 russet potatoes, washed and peeled

Peanut oil, or other neutral oil (enough to fill your deep skillet or frying pan with 2 inches/5 cm of oil)

Red chile powder (or store-bought chili powder), for seasoning

Salt, for seasoning

1 Slice the potatoes into super-thin round slices. They should be a consistent thickness, otherwise some will cook too fast.

2 Fill a large mixing bowl with ice water and soak the potato slices for about 10 minutes. Meanwhile, preheat the oil in the skillet over medium-high heat.

3 Transfer the potato slices to a clean, dry kitchen towel. Lay them out so they're not clumped together and pat them dry. Make sure they're quite dry—you don't want to add water to hot oil! Deep-frying can be *very* dangerous. Please exercise caution.

4 Drop the dry potato slices into the oil and let cook for 1 minute before stirring. Then, stir gently and often, making sure to press them down so they are fully submerged in the oil. Fry until golden brown and crispy—1½ to 2 minutes.

5 Use the slotted spoon or straining spoon to lift the chips out of the oil and onto a paper towel–lined plate. Quickly transfer them to a clean mixing bowl and, while they're still hot, dust with chile powder and salt, tossing them to coat with seasoning. Taste and add more seasoning, if desired.

Note: Homemade chips can get soft after a while. They can be re-crisped for 10 minutes in a 400°F (205°C) oven.

DEVILED EGGS WITH A KICK

MAKES 12 DEVILED EGGS

I love deviled eggs. I've been eating them my entire life, usually at family functions and special occasions. We seem to save this indulgence until there is something to celebrate, but deviled eggs can be made in advance of a barbeque and are a great accompaniment to burgers.

Every year I bring a plate of my spicy deviled eggs to my mother's Easter brunch, egg hunt, and bonnet contest (everyone shows up with a handmade bonnet, and my sister, Mary Beth, regularly walks away with the top prize). The recipe that I learned way back was my mother's, which was based on the simplest of elements: perfectly boiled eggs, good mayonnaise, Dijon mustard, and a sprinkle of paprika. She still refuses to put salt in the recipe because, she says, "the mayo has plenty of salt in it." With my mother, nothing is measured, and the finger-in-the-batter taste test says it all.

Over the years I've slightly corrupted my mother's basic recipe (with her blessing, of course). In mine, the combination of Dijon, sriracha, and pickled jalapeño creates a fairly complex heat profile, one that makes you reach for a second deviled egg . . . and a third.

EQUIPMENT

A medium-size stockpot
A strainer
A medium-size mixing bowl
A plastic zip-top bag

INGREDIENTS

6 large eggs
¼ cup (60 ml) mayonnaise
2 tablespoons mustard
1 tablespoon sriracha chili sauce
Pinch of salt
Paprika, for garnishing
Pickled Jalapeños (page 290)

1 Place the eggs in the stockpot and cover with lukewarm water. Bring to a gentle boil and cook for 1 minute. Cover, turn off the heat, and let sit for 10 minutes.

2 Prepare a bowl of ice water. Drain the eggs and transfer them to the ice water to prevent them from cooking further.

3 Once cool, peel the eggs and cut them in half lengthwise. Gently remove the yolks and add them to the mixing bowl. Place the egg whites on a serving plate.

4 Crumble the yolks with a fork, then add the mayo, mustard, and sriracha and stir or whisk until combined. It's okay if the filling is a little lumpy.

5 Add the filling to a plastic zip-top bag, seal the bag, cut the tip off of one of the corners of the bag, and squirt the mixture into the egg-white halves.

6 Dust each deviled egg with a pinch of salt and a dash of paprika and top with a pickled jalapeño slice just before serving.

THE WITCH DOCTOR

MAKES 1 DRINK

This is a weird one, but for the record, it totally works. It's also been on the menu for more than sixty years at North Carolina's very own regional chain What-A-Burger (not to be confused with the Texas Whataburger; the two chains legally coexist). Sixty years on a menu is legendary, and the Witch Doctor's longevity can be attributed to its large, multigenerational fanbase. A North Carolina native once told me "It tastes like home."

If you've ever gone around the world at the self-serve soda fountain at a restaurant or gas station, you know where we are going here. It's the thing you did as a kid where you filled a cup with ice then took a little bit from each soda dispenser (never diet though, yuck). And to be honest, not sure who I'm kidding here, I still do it. Though today my tastes are slightly more refined—I don't take ALL the sodas, just the Dr Pepper and Sprite. And obviously I've taught my kids and they too love to take their sodas around the world.

Some call it Suicide, and I've heard a Canadian friend call it Swamp Water.

But in this case, we are going around the world on a typical Tar Heel State fountain that is stocked with very specific, regional sodas—Cheerwine (the classic cherry soda from North Carolina), Lemon Sun Drop, Cherry Lemon Sun Drop, Dr Pepper, and Pepsi. Then, to make it a true Witch Doctor, you'll need to add a wedge of lemon and a handful of dill pickle chips. This wacked-out drink probably works because the salinity of the pickles cuts the sweetness, and the splash of garlicy brine creates a strange balance. It must be served over ice and enjoyed ice cold. Don't ever make the mistake I made once—I absentmindedly took a big swig of a melted, warm Witch Doctor about two hours later, driving down the road in the peak of summer. And I almost hurled on the dashboard.

EQUIPMENT

A large glass

A straw (important)

INGREDIENTS

Ice

Lemon Sun Drop soda

Cherry Lemon Sun Drop soda

Dr Pepper

Pepsi

Lemon wedges

Dill pickle chips

Some brine from the pickle jar

1 Fill the glass to the brim with ice.

2 Add equal splashes of each of the 4 sodas, squeeze in a lemon wedge, and float a few dill pickle chips on top.

3 Throw a splash of pickle brine in, insert straw, stir, and drink. (You need the straw because if you simply sip from the glass all you will get is pickle, and you will be sad and put the drink down.)

THE BEET BURGER

(FROM KORZO OF BROOKLYN, NEW YORK)

Let me make one thing perfectly clear—I do not like veggie burgers. I don't like the idea of them, I don't like the taste of them, and I consider them to be an insult to the word "burger." I actually love veggies in all forms: cooked, steamed, smoked, grilled, roasted, even in a cold-pressed juice. I'm a fairly healthy guy who loves cheeseburgers, and I have a great relationship with veggies. I fully understand that some people can't eat beef, or choose not to, and that's OK. Naturally, some of these people would still like to enjoy the hamburger "experience": the cheese, the toasted bun, those toppings, but just because it's on a bun does not make it a burger.

The real issue I have with veggie burgers is simply that they taste awful most of the time. They are either overprocessed, cardboard-stiff, soy-protein patties that taste like fake or frozen beef (which confuses me to no end. Why would the soy-protein people create a burger that mimics the worst burger you could eat?), or they are house-made gloppy, hot, veggie-and-bean mush pies. To add insult to injury, these mushy orbs are usually served on ridiculous, dried-out, oversize, sprouted wheat buns in the name of healthy eating. Gross.

But then I met the Beet Burger.

My friends Maria and Otto Zizak, who run the celebrated Brooklyn Slovakian outpost Korzo, have a firm understanding of what it takes to make and serve great food. Everything that leaves the kitchen has been thoroughly considered, made from the best ingredients, and served with love. Korzo does not function in a trendy locally sourced, artisanal way, but in an old-world European way (with artisanal, locally sourced ingredients) because that's the way it should be done. And if that's not enough, when the Slovakian president shows up at the consulate in Manhattan, it's Maria who cooks for him and his delegation.

Korzo is also home to one of my favorite (beef) burgers: a grilled burger that has been wrapped in Hungarian langos dough and tossed in the deep fryer (see Korzo's Deep-Fried Lángos Burger, page 210). The result is, well, you can use your burger-magination for this one. Langos bread when fried is heavenly and almost donut-like.

Beets are a staple in the mountainous regions of eastern Europe. In Slovakia, root vegetables like potatoes, beets, and horseradish are plentiful. Maria and Otto have incorporated beets into the Korzo menu in various forms, but the king of all is the Beet Burger. Korzo may have been the first to make a burger with beets in New York City, but today they have much company.

The Korzo Beet Burger is made with walnuts, black-eyed peas, garlic, and both raw and roasted beets. Roasting caramelizes and brings out the natural sugars in the beets. "We never boil beets at Korzo," Otto once pointed out. "Because then it would taste like hospital food." Add cheese and onions to the final product and you'll have one earthy, "beefy," damn-tasty burger, and the only one in its category that I will consume.

THE BEET BURGER

MAKES 8 TO 10 BURGERS

EQUIPMENT

Aluminum foil

A food processor

A large mixing bowl

A nonstick baking sheet (or a baking
sheet plus a silicone liner)

THE BURGER

1 large beet, peeled for roasting

30 ounces (850 grams) canned black-
eyed peas, drained and rinsed

4 cups (400 g) walnuts, soaked overnight in water and drained

2 medium carrots, peeled and shredded in a food processor with a shredding attachment

1 large raw beet, peeled and shredded

2 cloves fresh garlic, minced

1 tablespoon Korzo Ale Mustard (or any
good, grainy mustard)

2 tablespoons Frank's RedHot cayenne
pepper sauce or similar hot sauce

1 cup (80 g) panko bread crumbs

Salt and black pepper, to taste

2 tablespoons salted butter

8 soft half-wheat or sturdy soft burger
rolls, toasted (see instructions,
page 33)

THE TOPPINGS

Caramelized Onions (page 54)

Sautéed Mushrooms (recipe follows)

8 slices high-quality cheddar cheese

1 Preheat the oven to 400°F (205°C). Rub the beet with olive oil and wrap in two layers of aluminum foil. Roast for 1½ hours, or until a knife slides easily all the way through. Let cool, chop into cubes, and set aside. Reduce the oven temperature to 375°F (190°C).

2 In a food processor, coarsely blend the black-eyed peas and transfer to a large mixing bowl. Chop the walnuts in the food processor until coarse and add to the mixing bowl with the peas.

3 Add the carrots, both the raw and roasted beets, the garlic, mustard, hot sauce, and bread crumbs to the same bowl and mix by hand until blended. Season with salt and pepper to taste. The mixture should be a thick, pasty consistency.

4 Form patties that are roughly ¼ inch (6 mm) thick (patties can be chilled and/or frozen for later use). These burgers will not shrink during cooking, so form patties that are close to the circumference of your buns.

5 Put the patties on the nonstick baking sheet (or baking sheet with a silicone baking liner) and roast for 45 minutes.

6 While the Beet Burgers cook, prepare the sautéed mushrooms and caramelized onions.

7 When the burgers are finished baking, remove them from the oven. Preheat the cast-iron skillet over medium heat and add a pat of butter. Brown each patty on both sides, flipping the burgers carefully so they don't fall apart. (This step is optional.)

8 Add a spoonful of sautéed mushrooms to the top of each burger followed by a slice of cheese. Cover, and continue to cook until the cheese is melted, about 2 minutes.

9 Transfer finished beet burgers to the toasted buns and top with the caramelized onions.

SAUTÉED MUSHROOMS
Makes more than enough to top 8 beet burgers

1 tablespoon butter
2 cups (120 g) sliced cremini mushrooms
½ cup (120 ml) dry white wine
Sea salt, to taste

1 Melt the butter in a saucepan over medium heat and add the mushrooms.
2 Cover and cook over medium heat until the mushrooms release their liquid.
3 Pour in the wine and raise the heat to high. When liquid in the pan is reduced, remove from the heat. Salt to taste and set aside until ready to use on your beet burgers.

ACKNOWLEDGMENTS

It was only after I agreed to write my first cookbook that I discovered how much work it would be. I relish a good challenge, but I knew I could not do it alone (no way). Major kudos have to go to my trusty testing and shooting team of Sydney Rey and Kristoffer Brearton. This book would not have been possible without them, period. Sydney kept the entire book process together, kept me on task, and became our "kitchen cop"—there was no sneaking an extra pinch of salt past her, everything had to be measured twice.

"Fear not thy onion."

And Kris made magic daily, shooting more than two thousand images of burgers and ingredients. At one point, after seeing the first round of Kris's work, Sydney remarked, "I guess it doesn't matter what we write." Thanks, you two. Big thanks as well to food stylist Nicole Bergman and photographer Doug Young for the portraits and "action" shots in the book, as well as a few choice burger images.

The updated version of this book adds the indispensable help of Deirdre Wells—my confidante, partner, and food stylist. Thank you, Dee. And Sydney returned to help me sort the crazy, once again (it's like riding a bike, right, Syd?). Also, huge thanks to Justin Bolois at First We Feast, who worked with me to sort out most of the histories, recipes, and new entries that first appeared on our show *Burger Scholar Sessions*. Thanks to Justin and Complex Media for being burger believers and helping to usher in a new generation of burger love and appreciation on YouTube.

The endless supply of fresh-ground 80/20 chuck for testing and shooting came from my good friends at Schweid & Sons, meatpackers who create some of the most consistently great-tasting ground beef around. It was a treat to have the best in fresh beef at our disposal for months.

Thanks also to Bill Berrien for sending us authentic Wisconsin bratwurst. Grassland Dairy sent perfect Wisconsin butter, and the authentic New Mexican green chile came from Linda at NewMexicoCatalog.com. The authentic frita rolls came from Marta at El Mago, and Organic Valley supplied us with the best organic yellow American cheese. Thanks also to Jason Ferguson at Big Spaceship, for naming our Swine and Cheese, Matt and Emily for napkin help, and Andrew Zimmern for penning the foreword.

I'm also grateful for the willingness of my burger heroes to share their recipes, a few secrets, methods, and photos with me. Thanks especially to Steve Christian at Christian's Tailgate; Rich Belfer at White Rose; Glenn Fieber at Solly's Grille; Bonnie and John Eckre at Santa Fe Bite; John Boyles from the former Mr. Fable's and Kewpee Hamburgs; Jim Flaniken at Steak 'n Shake; the Gokey Family at Pete's Hamburgers; Eddie Sullivan at Brennan & Carr; Tony Moravec at Zaharakos; Mary, Dr. Phil, and Chef Michael Ollier at Certified Angus Beef®; Dana Browning at White Castle; Maria and Otto Zizak at Korzo; Klaus Wittrup in Denmark; Jimmy Hurlston in Australia; Chester Murray and George Degner in Quogue; and one of the biggest burger nerds of them all—my friend Tom Ryan at Smashburger.

And thanks, as well, to friends and family who have supported my burger craziness over the past two decades, and to the passionate burger fans and Expert Burger Tasters who have helped point me to my next great regional burger experience. All of this help and advice has shaped a vision that I believed in from the start, a vision that could not have been realized without your continued support.

This book would not have seen publication had it not been for two very important friends—my agent Laura Dail and publisher Michael Sand at Abrams. Laura has believed in my hamburger quest since the very beginning (almost two decades now), and when everyone else said I was nuts, she knew better. Thank you, Laura. And it has been dreamy working with the even-keeled publisher and editor Michael Sand. Thank you for your seemingly effortless guidance. And a big thanks to everyone at Abrams, including designer Danielle Youngsmith.

My mother continues to give me the confidence to get in the kitchen, keep things simple, and attempt to make magic. She really does make it look easy. Because of her the kitchen is my comfort zone. Thanks, Mom.

Finally, thank you to my two amazing children, Ruby and Mac, who have only known a dad who is crazy about burgers. It's for you that I make an effort to lead a semi-healthy life, with a balanced diet that includes many veggies, smoothies, and as much exercise as possible. Left to my own devices I'd probably burger my way to oblivion, which doesn't sound half bad.

INDEX

Page references in *italics* refer to photographs

A

American cheese, 24, 25, *25*
  The Bierock, 98–101, *99,*
    102–3
  The Carolina Slaw Burger,
    198–200, *201*
  The Chester-Rouer, 224–27,
    228–29
  The Deep-Fried Burger,
    186–89, *190–91*
  The Fluff Screamer, 204–7,
    207–9
  The Fried-Onion Burger,
    154–56, *157*
  The Gargiulo Burger, 218–21,
    222–23
  The Gom Cheese Brr-Grr,
    68–70, *71*
  The Griddle-Smashed Classic
    Cheeseburger, 30–33,
    34–35
  The Jersey Burger, 236–39,
    240–41
  The Jucy Lucy, 62–65, *66–67*
  The Pastrami Burger, 142–45,
    145, 146–47
  The Sloppy Burger, 260–63,
    264–65
  The Theta Special, 150–52,
    153
Angus Beef®, 21, *334–35,*
  334–35
Australia, 272–73
avocado
  The Bacon-Avocado Toast
    Burger, 114–16, *117*

B

bacon, 42–45, *46–47*
  The Bacon-Avocado Toast
    Burger, 114–16, *117*

Bacon in the Round, 294–95,
  295
  Burger with the Lot, 248,
    272–76, *277*
  Korzo's Deep-Fried Lángos
    Burger, 210–15, *211, 215–17*
  Steve's Country-Fried Bacon,
    280–81, *282–83*
  The Swine And Cheese, 164–
    67, *165, 168–69*
barbecue sauce, 150–52, *153*
  Burger with the Lot, 248,
    272–76, *277*
  Homemade BBQ Sauce,
    160–61, *162–63*
Bartley, Bill, 22, *25*
Basic Red Chile Sauce, 136–39,
  140–41
Beanless Beef Chili Sauce
  The Carolina Slaw Burger,
    198–200, *201*
  recipe, 284–85, *285*
beans. See also Frijoles Refritos
  de Jorge
  The Beet Burger, 320–23,
    324–25
  The San Antonio Beanburger,
    170–73, *174–75*
beef cuts and sourcing, 20–21,
  21, 334–35, 334–35
beef tallow, about, 18, 186–87
beer, 58, *59, 60–61*
beets
  The Beet Burger, 320–23,
    324–25
  Burger with the Lot, 248,
    272–76, *277*
beets, pickled
  The Bøfsandwich, 250–53,
    254–55
Belfer, Rich, 236–37, *237*

bell peppers
  Depression-Era Cole Slaw,
    306, *307*
  Mama's Potato Salad, 310–11,
    311–13
  Screamer Sauce, 204–7,
    207–9
  The Bierock, 98–101, *99, 102–3*
black-eyed peas, 320–23,
  324–25
The Bøfsandwich, 250–53,
  254–55
Boo Koo Hamburgers (Texas),
  31, *31*
Brader John (Malaysia), 261,
  261
bratwurst, 73
  The Sheboygan Brat Burger,
    72–75, *76–77*
Brazil, 266–67
breadcrumbs, 176–78, *179,*
  320–23, *324–25*
Brennan and Carr (New York),
  218–19, *219*
Bristol, Matt, 62
buns, 22–23, *23*
  Cuban rolls, 180–83, *184–85*
  Italian bread, 242, *243,*
    244–45
  Kaiser rolls, 72–75, *76–77,*
    218–21, *222–23,* 230–33,
    234–35
  potato rolls, 298–300, *299,*
    301
  toasting, 33
burger history, 10–13, *13,* 24,
  30–31, *31,* 142–43, *143,*
  249
burger map, 48–49, *48–49*
Burger-Perfect Fried Eggs,
  292–93, *293*

burger stands and street vendors, 180
  Brazilian, 266–67
  Greek, 142–43
  history, 30–31, 31, 143, 143
  Illinois, 51, 53, 53
  Malaysian, 260–61, 261, 292
  Wisconsin, 78–79, 79
Burger with the Lot, 248, 272–76, 277
butcher, sourcing from, 20–21, 21, 334–35, 334–35
butter, 292–93, 293
  The Butter Burger, 82–85, 86–87
buttermilk, 280–81, 282–83

C
cabbage
  The Bierock, 98–101, 99, 102–3
  The Carolina Slaw Burger, 198–200, 201
  Depression-Era Cole Slaw, 306, 307
  Stupid-Easy Cole Slaw, 308, 309
California, 110–11, 111, 114–15, 115, 142–43, 143, 284
Caramelized Onions
  The Beet Burger, 320–23, 324–25
  The Bøfsandwich, 250–53, 254–55
  Burger with the Lot, 248, 272–76, 277
  The Chicago Char Cheddar, 52–55, 56–57
  The Classic Patty Melt, 110–12, 113
  The Gargiulo Burger, 218–21, 222–23
  recipe, 55
The Carolina Slaw Burger, 198–200, 201
carrots
  The Beet Burger, 320–23, 324–25
  Stupid-Easy Cole Slaw, 308, 309

cast-iron cookware, 16, 16, 17, 30
celery, 298–300, 299, 301, 310–11, 311–13
charcoal grills/grilling, 18, 19. See also smoker
  Burger with the Lot, 248, 272–76, 277
  The Flame-Grilled Burger, 36–39, 37, 40–41
  The Sheboygan Brat Burger, 72–75, 76–77
cheddar, 24
  The Beet Burger, 320–23, 324–25
  Burger with the Lot, 248, 272–76, 277
  Cheeseburger Stuffing, 298–300, 299, 301
  Chef Joe Schweska's Original Sauce, 58, 59, 60–61, 61
  The Chicago Char Cheddar, 52–55, 56–57
  The Green Chile Cheeseburger, 130–33, 131, 134–35
  Mama's Pimena Cheese, 192–95, 195–97
  Motz's Whiz Cheese Spread, 170–73, 173–75
  The Steamed Cheeseburg, 230–33, 234–35
  The Swine And Cheese, 164–67, 165, 168–69
  The Tortilla Burger, 136–39, 140–41
cheese. See also American cheese
  cold pack, about, 52–53
  cream, 192–95, 195–97
  Emmentaler, 210–15, 211, 215–17
  mozzarella, 266–69, 270–71
  provolone, 242, 243, 244–45
  selecting and melting, 24–25, 25
  Swiss, 110–12, 113
Cheeseburger Stuffing, 298–300, 299, 301
Chef Joe Schweska's Original

Sauce, 58, 59, 60–61, 61
The Chester-Rouer, 224–27, 228–29
The Chester Special, 224, 227, 227
The Chicago Char Cheddar, 52–55, 56–57
chiles. See also The Green Chile Cheeseburger; red chiles
  chipotle, 288–89, 289
  Screamer Sauce, 204–7, 207–9
chili powder
  Beanless Beef Chili Sauce, 284–85, 285
  The Gom Cheese Brr-Grr, 68–70, 71
Christian, Steve, 280, 290
The Classic Patty Melt, 110–12, 113
Classic Utah Fry Sauce, 142–45, 145, 146–47
coleslaw
  Depression-Era Cole Slaw, 306, 307
  Stupid-Easy Cole Slaw, 308, 309
Connecticut, 12–13, 231, 231
cooking methods and tips, 10
  basics, 24–27, 27
  deep-frying, 61, 186–87, 296
  meat grinder and, 20–21, 166–67, 168
  outdoor grill, 36–37, 37, 39, 40
  smashing patties and, 30–31
  tools, 14–16, 14–19, 18, 20, 158–59
coriander, 256–59, 257, 259
corn
  The X-Tudo Burger, 266–69, 270–71
Country-Fried Bacon Cheeseburger, 280–81, 282–83
cream, 170–73, 174–75
cream cheese
  Mama's Pimena Cheese, 192–95, 195–97
Crown Burger (Utah), 142–43

The Cuban Frita, 180–83, 181, 184–85
cumin, 263, 263
curry powder, 263, 263

D

Danish Remoulade, 253, 253
Davis, Ross, 154
deep-frying, 314
    art of, 61, 186–87, 296
    The Deep-Fried Burger, 186–89, 190–91
    Korzo's Deep-Fried Lángos Burger, 210–15, 211, 215–17
DeForest, Thomas, 284
Denmark, 250–51, 251
Depression-Era Cole Slaw, 306, 307
Deviled Eggs with a Kick, 316–17, 317
dill, 302–3, 303
dough
    The Bierock, 98–101, 99, 102–3
    Korzo's Deep-Fried Lángos Burger, 210–15, 211, 215–17
Duke's Grill (North Carolina), 198–99, 199
Dyer's (Tennessee), 186–87, 187

E

Eastside Big Tom (Washington), 286
Eckre, Bonnie, 306
eggs
    Burger-Perfect Fried Eggs, 292–93, 293
    Burger with the Lot, 248, 272–76, 277
    Deviled Eggs with a Kick, 316–17, 317
    The Loco Moco, 118, 119, 120–21
    Mama's Potato Salad, 310–11, 311–13
    The Sloppy Burger, 260–63, 264–65
    The X-Tudo Burger, 266–69, 270–71

F

Fieber, Glenn, 83, 85
The Flame-Grilled Burger, 36–39, 37, 40–41
Florida, 180–81
The Fluff Screamer, 204–7, 207–9
The Fried-Onion Burger, 154–56, 157
Fried Onion Hay
    The Bøfsandwich, 250–53, 254–55
    recipe, 296–97, 297
fries, 13, 236. See also Thin-Cut Fried Potatoes
    The Horseshoe Sandwich, 58, 59, 60–61
Frijoles Refritos de Jorge
    recipe, 173
    The San Antonio Beanburger, 170–73, 174–75
    The Tortilla Burger, 136–39, 140–41
Fritos, 170–73, 174–75
Fritsch, Chuck, 286

G

The Gargiulo Burger, 218–21, 222–23
Geist, Ralph, 150
Germans, 12, 72, 98, 210, 250
ginger, 122, 123, 124–25
Glenn's Stewed Onions, My Way, 82–85, 86–87
Gokey family, 78–79
The Gom Cheese Brr-Grr, 68–70, 71
Goop Sauce, 286–87, 287
Gravy, Super-Easy Tasty Brown, 118, 119, 120–21, 299, 300
Great Depression, 13, 176, 306
Greeks, 142–43
The Green Chile Cheeseburger, 130–33, 131, 134–35
The Griddle-Smashed Classic Cheeseburger, 30–33, 34–35
grilling. See charcoal grills/grilling; smoker
grinding meat, 20–21, 164–67,

168
The Guberburger, 104–6, 107
Gyro II (New York), 302–3, 303

H

ham
    The X-Tudo Burger, 266–69, 270–71
Hamburger America (book and film), 10, 82, 104–5, 266, 280
Hamburger Inn (Oklahoma), 154–55, 155
The Hamburger Parm, 242, 243
The Hamburger Parm, 244–45
Harry's Schnäck Sauce, 288–89, 289
The Hat (California), 142, 143, 143
Hawaii, 118, 122
Hawk, Harry, 288
Homemade BBQ Sauce, 160–61, 162–63
horseradish, 253, 253
The Horseshoe Sandwich, 58, 59, 60–61
hot dogs
    Screamer Sauce, 204–7, 207–9
hot sauce. See also sriracha
    Beanless Beef Chili Sauce, 284–85, 285
    The Beet Burger, 320–23, 324–25
    The Gom Cheese Brr-Grr, 68–70, 71
    Motz's Kinda-Secret Frita Sauce, 180–83, 184–85
    Screamer Sauce, 204–7, 207–9
Howard's Famous (California), 114, 115, 115

I

Illinois, 13, 13, 51, 53, 53, 58
Indiana, 68–69, 69
international burgers, about, 11, 249
Iowa, 88–89, 89
The Islak, 256–59, 257, 259

The Italian Burger
(Massachusetts), 242

J
Jack's Lunch (Connecticut),
231, 231
jalapeños. See Pickled Jalapeños
The Jersey Burger, 236–39,
240–41
J.G. Melon (New York), 8–9, 42,
43, 43
Joe Rouer's Bar (Wisconsin),
225, 225
The Jucy Lucy, 62–65, 66–67

K
Kansas, 98
Katsanevas, James and Mike,
142–43
ketchup, 272–76, 277
Classic Utah Fry Sauce, 142–
45, 145, 146–47
Homemade BBQ Sauce,
160–61, 162–63
Kewpee Hotel Hamburgs
(Michigan), 92–93, 93
Korn, Matt, 126–27
Korzo (New York)
The Beet Burger, 320–23,
324–25
Korzo's Deep-Fried Lángos
Burger, 210–15, 211, 215–17
restaurant, 210, 320–21

L
Latham's Hamburger Inn
(Mississippi), 177, 177
Leland Hotel (Illinois), 58
The Loco Moco, 118, 119,
120–21
The Loose Meat Sandwich,
88–90, 91
Louis' Lunch (Connecticut),
12–13

M
Macho Tostada (Texas), 170
Madrid, Chris, 170
Maggi seasoning, 261–63,
264–65

Malaysia, 260–61, 261, 292
Mama (mother of Motz), 11, 16,
284
Mama's Pimena Cheese,
192–95, 195–97
Mama's Potato Salad, 310–11,
311–13
map, burger, 48–49, 48–49
Marshmallow Fluff
The Fluff Screamer, 204–7,
207–9
Massachusetts, 242
Matt's Bar (Minnesota), 62–63,
63
Matt's Place Drive-In
(Montana), 126–27, 127
mayonnaise
Classic Utah Fry Sauce, 142–
45, 145, 146–47
Danish Remoulade, 253, 253
Goop Sauce, 286–87, 287
Harry's Schnäck Sauce, 288–
89, 289
Kewpie, 122, 123, 124–25,
261–63, 264
Mama's Pimena Cheese,
192–95, 195–97
Miracle Whip, 126–28, 129
Mr. Fables-Style or Olive-
Mayo Mixes, 94, 96–97
Stupid-Easy Cole Slaw, 308,
309
The White Sauce, 302–3, 303
meat grinder, 20–21, 164–67,
168
Merkts cheddar spread, 52–55,
56–57
Michigan, 92–95, 93, 96
Minnesota, 62–63, 63
Miracle Whip, 126–28, 129
Mississippi, 176–77, 177
Missouri, 104–5, 105
Mr. Fables (Michigan), 92–95,
96
Mo Club (Montana), 42, 43, 43
molasses, 68–70, 71, 160–61,
162–63
Montana, 42, 43, 43, 126–27,
127
Moravec, Tony, 68–69

Motz's Kinda-Secret Frita
Sauce, 180–83, 184–85
Motz's Whiz Cheese Spread,
170–73, 173–75
Murray, Chester, 224, 227, 227
Mushrooms, Sautéed, 320–23,
324–25
mustard
The Beet Burger, 320–23,
324–25
Deviled Eggs with a Kick,
316–17, 317
Goop Sauce, 286–87, 287
Harry's Schnäck Sauce, 288–
89, 289
Homemade BBQ Sauce,
160–61, 162–63
Stupid-Easy Cole Slaw, 308,
309
My Red Sauce
The Hamburger Parm, 242,
243, 244–45
The Islak, 256–59, 257, 259
recipe, 245, 245

N
Naylor, William Wallace, 110
Nebraska, 98
New Jersey, 236–37, 237
New Mexico, 130–31, 136–39,
137, 306
New York, 8–9, 42–43, 43, 218–
19, 219, 224, 288, 302–3,
303. See also Korzo
North Carolina, 177, 198–99,
199, 318
nuts
The Beet Burger, 320–23,
324–25
The Guberburger, 104–6, 107
The Nutburger, 126–28, 129

O
Oklahoma, 150–51, 151, 154–55,
155
olives
The Olive Burger, 92–95,
96–97
Smoked Olives, 161
Ollier, Michael, 36–37, 39

onion. See also Caramelized
Onions
Cheeseburger Stuffing, 298–
300, 299, 301
The Chester-Rouer, 224–27,
228–29
The Cuban Frita, 180–83, 181,
184–85
The Fluff Screamer, 204–7,
207–9
The Fried-Onion Burger,
154–56, 157
Fried Onion Hay, 296–97,
297
Glenn's Stewed Onions, My
Way, 82–85, 86–87
The Gom Cheese Brr-Grr,
68–70, 71
The Islak, 256–59, 257, 259
The Jersey Burger, 236–39,
240–41
The Loco Moco, 118, 119,
120–21
The Poached Burger, 78–80,
81
Oscar's Bøf Bar (Denmark),
250–51, 251

P
The Pantry Restaurant (New
Mexico), 136–37, 137
paprika
The Cuban Frita, 180–83, 181,
184–85
The Islak, 256–59, 257, 259
Super-Secret Sloppy
Seasoning, 263, 263
paprika, smoked, 114–16, 117
Paradise Pup (Illinois), 51, 53,
53
parchment paper, 18, 18, 269
The Pastrami Burger, 142–45,
145, 146–47
peanuts/peanut butter
The Guberburger, 104–6, 107
The Nutburger, 126–28, 129
Pennsylvania, 204–5, 205
Pete's Hamburgers (Wisconsin),
78–79, 79
Pickled Jalapeños

Deviled Eggs with a Kick,
316–17, 317
recipe, 290–91, 291
pickles, 286–87, 287
Danish Remoulade, 253, 253
Mama's Potato Salad, 310–11,
311–13
The Witch Doctor, 318–19,
319
The Pimento Cheeseburger,
192–95, 196–97
pineapple
Burger with the Lot, 248,
272–76, 277
The Poached Burger, 78–80, 81
pork gravy
The Bøfsandwich, 250–53,
254–55
pork roll, Taylor
The Jersey Burger, 236–39,
240–41
potatoes. See also fries; Thin-
Cut Fried Potatoes
Mama's Potato Salad, 310–11,
311–13
Red Chile Potato Chips,
314–15, 315
Ptomaine Tommy's (California),
284

R
red chiles
Basic Red Chile Sauce, 136–
39, 140–41
Red Chile Potato Chips,
314–15, 315
El Rey de las Fritas (Florida),
180–81
rice
The Loco Moco, 118, 119,
120–21
roast beef
The Gargiulo Burger, 218–21,
222–23
Rouer, Joe, 225, 225
rye bread, 110–12, 113

S
The San Antonio Beanburger,
170–73, 174–75

sauces. See toppings and sauces
sausage. See bratwurst
Sautéed Mushrooms, 320–23,
324–25
Schnäck (New York), 288
Schweska, Joe, 58, 60–61
Screamer Sauce, 204–7, 207–9
seasonings. See also specific
seasonings
Seasoned Salt Substitute, 281
Super-Secret Sloppy
Seasoning, 263, 263
The Sheboygan Brat Burger,
72–75, 76–77
Sill's Snack Shack (Texas),
170–71, 171
The Sloppy Burger, 260–63,
264–65
Slovakians, 210–11, 320–21
The Slug Burger, 176–78, 179
smoker, 159
The Smoked Burger, 158–61,
162–63
Smoked Olives, 161
Snappy Lunch (North
Carolina), 177
soda (beverage)
The Witch Doctor, 318–19,
319
Solly's Grille (Wisconsin),
82–83, 83
sour cream, 286–87, 287
South Carolina, 192–93
soy sauce, 122, 123, 124–25
Split-T (Oklahoma), 150–51, 151
sriracha
Deviled Eggs with a Kick,
316–17, 317
Mama's Pimena Cheese,
192–95, 195–97
The Sloppy Burger, 260–63,
264–65
The Steamed Cheeseburg, 230–
33, 234–35
Steve's Country-Fried Bacon,
280–81, 282–83
street vendors. See burger
stands and street vendors
Stupid-Easy Cole Slaw
The Carolina Slaw Burger,

198–200, 201
  recipe, 308, 309
Super-Easy Tasty Brown Gravy,
  118, 119, 120–21, 299, 300
Super-Secret Sloppy Seasoning,
  263, 263
sweet relish, 286–87, 287
The Swine And Cheese, 164–67,
  165, 168–69

T

Taylor pork roll, 236–39,
  240–41
Taylor's Maid-Rite (Iowa),
  88–89, 89
Ted's Restaurant (Connecticut),
  231
Tennessee, 186–87, 187
The Teriyaki Burger, 122, 123,
  124–25
Texas, 31, 31, 158–59, 164–65,
  170–71, 171, 280, 290
The Theta Special, 150–52, 153
The Thick Pub Classic Burger,
  42–45, 46–47
Thin-Cut Fried Potatoes
  The Cuban Frita, 180–83, 181,
    184–85
  recipe, 183
  The X-Tudo Burger, 266–69,
    270–71
Tiny Naylor's Drive-In
  (California), 110, 111, 111
tomatoes, canned and sauced,
  180–83, 184–85. See also
  My Red Sauce
  Beanless Beef Chili Sauce,
    284–85, 285
  The Gom Cheese Brr-Grr,
    68–70, 71
  Screamer Sauce, 204–7,
    207–9
Tony's Lunch (Pennsylvania),
  204, 205, 205
Tookie's Hamburgers (Texas),
  164–65
tools, 14–16, 14–19, 18, 20,
  158–59
toppings and sauces. See
  also barbecue sauce;

Worcestershire
  Bacon in the Round, 294–95,
    295
  Basic Red Chile Sauce, 136–
    39, 140–41
  Beanless Beef Chili Sauce,
    284–85, 285
  Burger-Perfect Fried Eggs,
    292–93, 293
  Chef Joe Schweska's Original
    Sauce, 58, 59, 60–61, 61
  Classic Utah Fry Sauce, 142–
    45, 145, 146–47
  Danish Remoulade, 253, 253
  Fried Onion Hay, 296–97,
    297
  Goop Sauce, 286–87, 287
  Harry's Schnäck Sauce, 288–
    89, 289
  Mama's Pimena Cheese,
    192–95, 195–97
  Merkts cheddar spread,
    52–55, 56–57
  Motz's Kinda-Secret Frita
    Sauce, 180–83, 184–85
  Motz's Whiz Cheese Spread,
    170–73, 173–75
  My Red Sauce, 245, 245
  Pickled Jalapeños, 290–91,
    291
  pork gravy, 250–53, 254–55
  Sautéed Mushrooms, 320–
    23, 324–25
  Super-Easy Tasty Brown
    Gravy, 118, 119, 120–21,
    299, 300
  Teriyaki Sauce and Marinade,
    122, 123, 124–25
The Tortilla Burger, 136–39,
  140–41
Turkey, 256–57

U

Utah, 143
  Classic Utah Fry Sauce, 142–
    45, 145, 146–47

W

walnuts
  The Beet Burger, 320–23,

324–25
Washington, 286
What-A-Burger (North
  Carolina), 318
Wheel Inn Drive-In (Missouri),
  104–5, 105
White Castle, 13, 13, 31, 249
White Rose (New Jersey),
  236–37, 237
The White Sauce, 302–3, 303
wine
  mirin, 122, 123, 124–25
  white, 55, 82–85, 86–87, 323
Wisconsin, 72–73, 73, 78–79,
  79, 82–83, 83, 225, 225
The Witch Doctor, 318–19, 319
Worcestershire, 160–61, 162–63
  Beanless Beef Chili Sauce,
    284–85, 285
  Danish Remoulade, 253, 253
  The Sloppy Burger, 260–63,
    264–65

X

The X-Tudo Burger, 266–69,
  270–71

Z

Zaharakos (Indiana), 68–69, 69
Zimmern, Andrew, 8–9
Zizak, Maria and Otto, 210, 211,
  212, 320–21

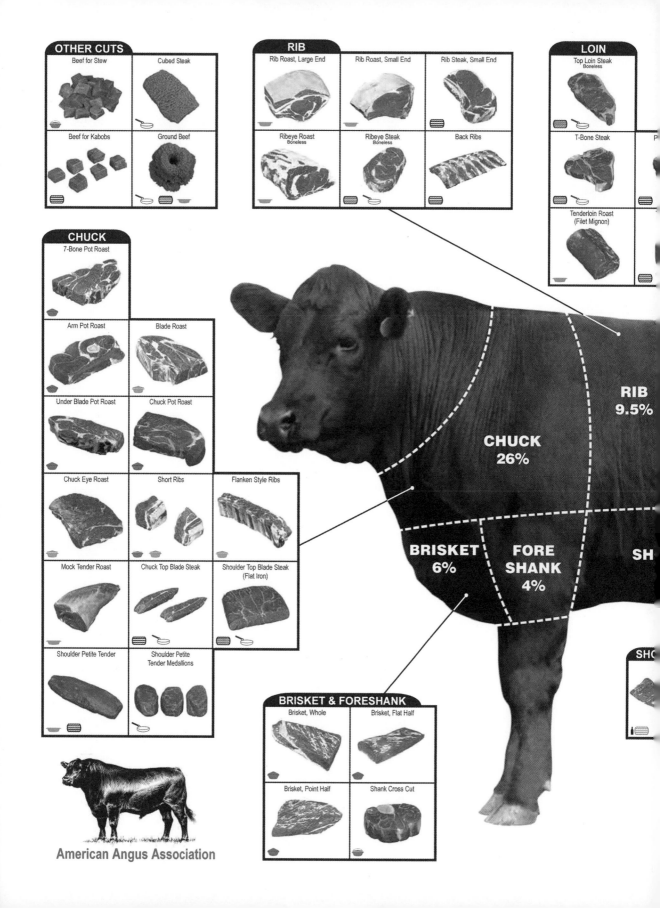

OTHER CUTS

Beef for Stew

Cubed Steak

Beef for Kabobs

Ground Beef

RIB

Rib Roast, Large End

Rib Roast, Small End

Rib Steak, Small End

Ribeye Roast
Boneless

Ribeye Steak
Boneless

Back Ribs

LOIN

Top Loin Steak
Boneless

T-Bone Steak

P

Tenderloin Roast
(Filet Mignon)

CHUCK

7-Bone Pot Roast

Arm Pot Roast

Blade Roast

Under Blade Pot Roast

Chuck Pot Roast

Chuck Eye Roast

Short Ribs

Flanken Style Ribs

Mock Tender Roast

Chuck Top Blade Steak

Shoulder Top Blade Steak
(Flat Iron)

Shoulder Petite Tender

Shoulder Petite
Tender Medallions

RIB
9.5%

CHUCK
26%

BRISKET
6%

**FORE
SHANK**
4%

SH

SHO

BRISKET & FORESHANK

Brisket, Whole

Brisket, Flat Half

Brisket, Point Half

Shank Cross Cut

American Angus Association

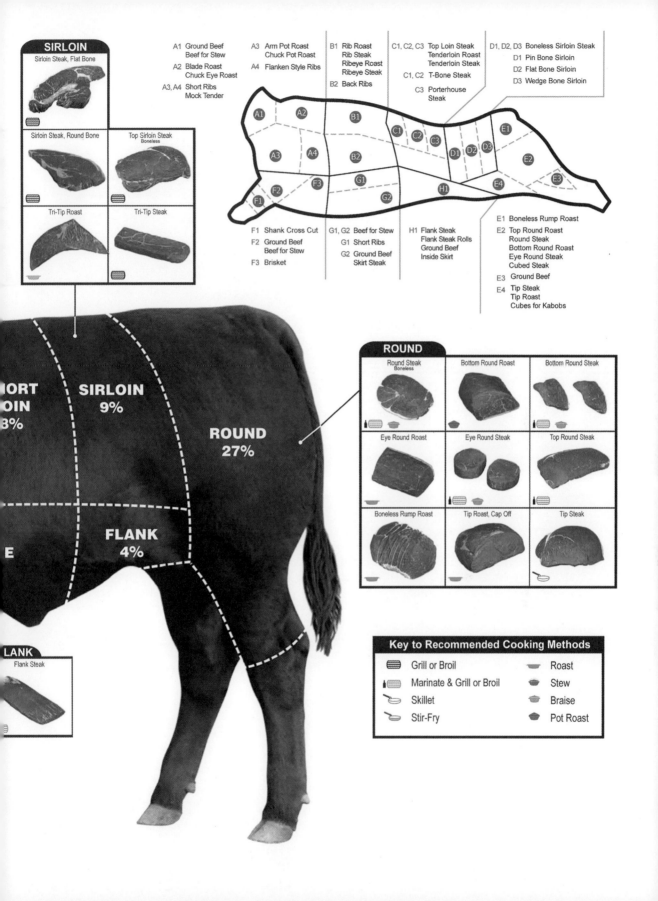

SIRLOIN

Sirloin Steak, Flat Bone

Sirloin Steak, Round Bone

Top Sirloin Steak
Boneless

Tri-Tip Roast

Tri-Tip Steak

A1 Ground Beef
   Beef for Stew
A2 Blade Roast
   Chuck Eye Roast
A3, A4 Short Ribs
   Mock Tender

A3 Arm Pot Roast
   Chuck Pot Roast
A4 Flanken Style Ribs

B1 Rib Roast
   Rib Steak
   Ribeye Roast
   Ribeye Steak
B2 Back Ribs

C1, C2, C3 Top Loin Steak
   Tenderloin Roast
   Tenderloin Steak
C1, C2 T-Bone Steak
C3 Porterhouse
   Steak

D1, D2, D3 Boneless Sirloin Steak
D1 Pin Bone Sirloin
D2 Flat Bone Sirloin
D3 Wedge Bone Sirloin

F1 Shank Cross Cut
F2 Ground Beef
   Beef for Stew
F3 Brisket

G1, G2 Beef for Stew
G1 Short Ribs
G2 Ground Beef
   Skirt Steak

H1 Flank Steak
   Flank Steak Rolls
   Ground Beef
   Inside Skirt

E1 Boneless Rump Roast
E2 Top Round Roast
   Round Steak
   Bottom Round Roast
   Eye Round Steak
   Cubed Steak
E3 Ground Beef
E4 Tip Steak
   Tip Roast
   Cubes for Kabobs

SHORT LOIN 8%
SIRLOIN 9%
ROUND 27%
FLANK 4%
FLANK
Flank Steak

ROUND

Round Steak
Boneless

Bottom Round Roast

Bottom Round Steak

Eye Round Roast

Eye Round Steak

Top Round Steak

Boneless Rump Roast

Tip Roast, Cap Off

Tip Steak

Key to Recommended Cooking Methods

Grill or Broil	Roast
Marinate & Grill or Broil	Stew
Skillet	Braise
Stir-Fry	Pot Roast

PHOTO CREDITS

All photographs by Kristoffer Brearton, Douglas Young, and George Motz, with the exception of the following: p. 13 courtesy White Castle, the White Castle images and materials and the "WHITE CASTLE®" mark are the exclusive property of White Castle Management Co. and are used under license; pp. 21 and 334–335 American Angus Association/Certified Angus Beef Brand; p. 27 Ruby Motz; p. 31 Russell Lee, Library of Congress, Prints & Photographs Division, FSA/OWI Collection; p. 69 courtesy Tony Moravec/Zaharakos Ice Cream Parlor and Museum; p. 73 courtesy Sheboygan County Historical Research Center; p. 83 courtesy Solly's Grille; pp. 93, 96 courtesy John Boyles; p. 105 courtesy John Brandkamp, Wheel Inn Drive-In; p. 108 (bottom left) courtesy Steak 'N Shake Enterprises; p. 111 courtesy Marc Wanamaker/Bison Archive; p. 115 Tim Fyke; p. 143 courtesy The Hat Restaurant; p. 151 courtesy Oklahoma Historical Society; p. 155 Quinta Scott, *Along Route 66*, University of Oklahoma Press, 2000; p. 181 courtesy Mercedes Alvarez, El Rey des las Fritas; p. 187 courtesy Dyer's Hamburgers; p. 205 courtesy Rolando Pujol; p. 227 courtesy Dee Wells; p. 231 courtesy Russell Library, Middletown, CT; p. 251 courtesy Oscars Bøfbar; p. 261 courtesy Mohd Adly Rizal, FriedChlillies Media; p. 311 courtesy Mary Thames Louis; p. 324 (bottom left + bottom middle) Sydney Rey

Kristoffer Brearton:
15 (right), 16–17, 23, 25, 28 (top left), 47, 66, 67, 91, 108 (bottom left), 81, 86, 87, 96 (except top left), 97, 102, 103, 107, 117, 123, 129 (bottom right), 140, 141, 147, 168, 169, 174, 175, 179, 184, 185, 190, 191, 193, 196, 197, 201, 234 (bottom right), 240, 241, 243, 278 (top right), 282, 283, 285, 287, 289, 295, 306, 309, 326

Douglas Young: 14, 15 (left), 16, 19, 27 (top right, + bottom right), 34, 35, 37, 40, 41, 46, 119, 129, 134 (bottom left + bottom right), 135, 146, 159 (right), 162, 163, 234, 235, 278 (bottom left + bottom right), 291, 293, 304 (middle left, bottom left, + bottom middle), 312, 313, 317

George Motz: 2, 4, 18, 28 (middle left), 43, 50 (top, middle, bottom right), 53, 56–57, 59, 61, 63, 71, 76–77, 79, 89, 99, 113, 127, 131, 134 (top left + top right), 137, 148 (top left, bottom right), 153, 157, 159 (left), 177, 202, 205, 207–209, 211, 215, 216–217, 222–223, 236, 246, 248, 251, 253, 254–255, 257, 259, 261, 263, 264–265, 270–271, 275, 278 (middle left), 297, 299, 301, 302 (top right + middle right), 303, 307 (bottom right), 315, 319, 325

Editor: Michael Sand
Designer: John Gall
Design Manager: Danielle Youngsmith
Managing Editor: Lisa Silverman
Production Manager: Larry Pekarek

Library of Congress Control Number: 2022945427

ISBN: 978-1-4197-6514-8
eISBN: 978-1-64700-850-5

Text copyright © 2016, 2023 George Motz
Map illustrations by Heesang Lee

Cover © 2023 Abrams

Printed and bound in China

10 9 8 7 6 5 4 3

Abrams books are available at special discounts when purchased in quantity for premiums and promotions as well as fundraising or educational use. Special editions an also be created to specification. For details, contact specialsales@abramsbooks.com or the address below.

Abrams® is a registered trademark of Harry N. Abrams, Inc.

ABRAMS The Art of Books
195 Broadway, New York, NY 10007
abramsbooks.com